A Menagerie
of
Brain Teasers

Compiled by
Alan Wareham

WARD LOCK

To Tracey

Copyright © text 1990 Alan Wareham
© Illustrations Ward Lock Limited 1990

First published 1990 by
Ward Lock, Villiers House,
41/47 Strand, London WC2N 5JE

A Cassell imprint

Designed by Chris Warren
Illustrations by Ian Foulis

Text set in Plantin
by Fakenham Photosetting Limited,
Fakenham, Norfolk
Printed and bound in Great Britain
by Cox & Wyman Ltd, Reading

British Library Cataloguing in Publication Data

Wareham, Alan
A Mensa book of brainteasers
1. Quiz games
I. Title
793.73

ISBN 0–7063–6427–0

CONTENTS

Acknowledgements

I wish to thank the British Mensa Committee, under the chairmanship of Sir Clive Sinclair, for agreeing to the publication of this book. Thanks also to British Mensa's Executive Director, Harold Gale, for his assistance with my application and to Ken Russell, for his helpful comments and advice. Thanks also to Kie MisKelly, Editor of *The Gazette* in South Shields, for whom my 'Fun Time' puzzle column was originally created, and to Peter Norman of Advance Features, for his help and advice in furthering my puzzle compiling throughout the UK and abroad. Last, but not least, a special thank you to my wife Tracey, not just for her help in checking the manuscript, puzzle solutions and clarifying instructions, but for her enthusiastic support and everlasting optimism.

INTRODUCTION

Mensa is more than just puzzles. An odd statement for the first sentence of an introduction to a Mensa book of brain teasers, but true. Before joining Mensa in 1985, I, like many other non-Mensans was under the impression that Mensa was a group of intelligent people who solved and set puzzles. Mensa is in fact an international organisation of some 100,000 members in 110 countries, within which there is a huge variety of special interest groups devoted to such varied subjects as artificial intelligence, humour, space, cricket, computers—and the solving and setting of puzzles! Members of Mensa are also encouraged to form special interest groups to suit their own particular interest if one does not already exist.

Mensa is a Latin word meaning 'table', implying a round table society where every member is equal. The only qualification for eligibility for membership of Mensa is that one attains a score within the upper two per cent of the general population, on an approved and supervised intelligence test.

Members of Mensa may express opinions as members of Mensa, but Mensa itself neither expresses or holds any ideological, philosophical, political or religious opinions. Mensa members come from a wide cross-section of the community, and inevitably express their own opinions on almost every subject, and indeed are encouraged to do so through the special interest groups, local, regional and national gatherings and through the *Mensa Journal*.

It was in fact in the *Mensa Journal* in which one of the first puzzles I compiled appeared in January 1987, on 'Ken Russell's New Year Puzzles' page. I have since compiled puzzles for various publications, and this led me to produce this book of brain teasers. The puzzles in this book are mostly more difficult than the type of puzzle you can expect to find in your average monthly puzzle magazine, but then again they are not impossible to solve. They have been arranged into sections of similar types of puzzles, with the exception of the warm-up section. Each section has been arranged so that the puzzles become progressively more difficult as you work your way through them. I have allocated a star-rating to each puzzle so that you can monitor your performance throughout the book as well as each section.

★ Easy
★★ Average
★★★ Challenging
★★★★ Difficult
★★★★★ Very difficult

The puzzles have been cross-referenced with two numbers, a question number (Q) and an answer number (A). This has been done so that when you check the answer to a puzzle, there is no risk of seeing the answer to the next one before you try and solve it. Before you start solving the puzzles, remember, they are only a small part of Mensa, and if you apply for membership, I wish you every success.

MENSA SOCIETIES

UK
British Mensa Ltd
Mensa House
St John's Square
Wolverhampton
WV2 4AH

AUSTRALIA
Australian Mensa Incorporated
P.O. Box 213
Toorak
Victoria 3142

CANADA
Mensa Canada Society
P.O. Box 505
Station "S"
Toronto
Ontario M5M 4L8

USA
American Mensa Ltd
2626 E14 Street
Brooklyn
N.Y. 11235

INTERNATIONAL
Mensa International Ltd
15 The Ivories
6–8 Northampton Street
London
N1 2HY

WARM-UPS

This section should 'warm-up' your brain before it is teased by the sections to follow. Most of the puzzles are one or two star-rated to ease you into the way in which my mind works, and the logical, or not so logical way in which they have been set. Remember, things are not always what they appear to be, but then again, they could be!

Q1 Cubes (A31)

★

Which two cubes from 1 to 6 cannot be made from the flattened cube?

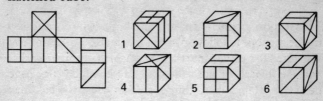

Q2 Letter boxes (A57)

In each of the grids below, fill in the missing boxes.

★
1

J	A	J	?
F	M	A	?
M	J	S	?

★★
2

A	C	L	?
A	G	P	?
C	L	S	?

Q3 Numbers (A2)

What is the next number in each of these sequences?
* ★   A) 15, 20, 20, 6, 6, 19, 19, 5, 14, 20, 5, ?
* ★   B) 1, 8, 11, 18, 80, ?
* ★   C) 1, 2, 4, 14, 21, 22, 24, 31, ?
* ★★   D) 4, 1, 3, 1, 2, 4, 3, ?
* ★★   E) 1, 2, 4, 7, 28, 33, 198, ?
* ★★   F) 17, 8, 16, 23, 28, 38, 49, 62, ?
* ★★   G) 27, 216, 279, 300, ?
* ★★   H) 9, 7, 17, 79, 545, ?
* ★★   I) 2, 3, 10, 12, 13, 20, ?
* ★★   J) 34, 58, 56, 60, 42, ?

9

Q4 Words (A69)

★★

1 COMPATIBLE is to CURIE as AUDIENCE is to which of the following:
FREQUENT   OCEANIC   ROADSIDE
UNDERGONE   UNSEEN

★★

2 SOUND = 188
HELD = 70
OFTEN = 177
CRAZY = 271
ANSWER = ?

Q5 Age old question (A50)

★★

Dave is younger than Fred and older than George.
Alan is younger than Ian and older than Colin.
Ian is younger than George and older than John.
John is younger than Colin and older than Edward.
Fred is younger than Barry and older than Harry.
Harry is older than Dave.
WHO IS THE YOUNGEST?

Q6 Missing letters (A20)

★★

What are the two missing letters?
? K O ? I N E F A

Q7 Logic path (A85)

★★

Starting at the letter L and working across the grid to the letter H, see how many different ways you can find of collecting the letters LOGICPATH in the correct order. You may move in any direction, one square at a time, and may only collect nine letters each time.

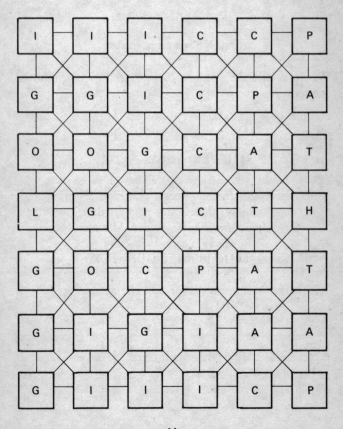

Q8 What next? (A12)

★★

What is the next letter in the following sequence?

U, A, R, H, E, U, ?

Q9 Letter sequence (A93)

★★

What is the next letter in the following sequence?

O E T E F E S N N E E ?

Q10 Sequence (A1)

★★

Where should the number 10 be placed to continue the sequence?

8 5 4 9 1 7 6 3 2

Q11 Two halves (A41)

★★

If the letters from A to M = 202, what do the letters from N to Z = ?

Q12 Number boxes (A26)

★★

Which box of numbers is the odd one out?

A

5	8	3
1	4	6
7	2	9

B

6	5	8
3	1	4
9	7	2

C

4	8	2
1	5	7
6	3	9

Q13 Letter sequence two (A105)

★★★

What is the next letter in this sequence?

A B H F M C I G T D O J U ?

Q14 Division (A77)

★★★★

Divide the grid below into four equal parts, each of which should be the same shape and contain 16 letters. The 16 letters should then be arranged to form a 16-letter word. Each of the four parts contains a different word.

L	I	B	N	C	I	S	C
H	I	I	I	E	O	R	I
E	I	I	M	S	M	E	I
R	R	E	S	P	P	N	N
N	U	P	M	A	R	U	T
S	E	O	N	T	D	O	A
B	S	S	I	N	N	O	D
L	Y	T	R	G	I	N	N

ANAGRAMS

Anagrams first appeared more than 2000 years ago when it was common practice among the Greeks to rearrange the letters in people's names to reveal their hidden characteristics. The thirteenth-century Jewish mystics known as the Cabbalists even believed that there were magical properties in the Hebrew alphabet, and that Jeremiah and other prophets created human beings out of dust by reciting letters in a particular order: one for male and another for female. The human beings ('golems') could then be turned back into dust by reciting the letters in reverse order.

The belief that rearranging letters of the alphabet had or created powers continued into the Renaissance. It was then thought that character or fate could be discovered by rearranging the letters of a person's name, making an anagram.

Louis XIII, King of France, even appointed a Royal Anagrammatist with a salary of £1200 a year. Before Charles Lutwidge Dodgson chose the name Lewis Carroll, which came from Lutwidge-Ludovic-Louis-Lewis, and Charles-Carolus-Carroll, he considered anagrams of Charles Lutwidge: Edgar Cuthwellis and Edgar U C Westhill. Lewis Carroll was fond of anagrams and devised this anagram of Florence Nightingale: Flit on, cheering angel. This is an example of the type of anagram which became prevalent in the nineteenth century, *i.e.* the anagram should be an appropriate description of the person or thing being anagrammed. Anagrams of persons or things which are the opposite of the original word or sentence are sometimes called antigrams.

Most of the anagrams contained in this section are one-word anagrams and have no connection in meaning with the anagrammed word. When solving anagrams I find it often helps by looking for word endings like ION, ING, LESS or NESS, and then form a word using the remaining letters. Some people write all of the letters down in a circle or in alphabetical order. Whatever method you employ, use your imagination and try not to be in too much of a hurry to look at the answers.

Q15   One-word one   (A60)

★★

All of the following are one-word anagrams:

1 Avertible	7 Immersing	13 Anacruses
2 Coastline	8 Adulation	14 Arsenical
3 Decimated	9 Antidotes	15 Continuer
4 Relatives	10 Argentine	16 Lancaster
5 Optically	11 Mobilises	17 Pignorate
6 Introduce	12 Gyrations	18 Analogist

Q16   One-word two   (A4)

★★

All of the following are one-word anagrams:

1 Acetamide	7 Acierated	13 Adminicle
2 Cretinoid	8 Grandiose	14 Catechism
3 Largition	9 Canoeists	15 Gradients
4 Esperanto	10 Bacterial	16 Alignment
5 Runcinate	11 Aniconism	17 Ceilinged
6 Savourily	12 Cognition	18 Inoculant

Q17   One-word three   (A71)

★★

All the following are one-word anagrams:

1 Excitation	6 Nutriments
2 Shattering	7 Alphametic
3 Neologisms	8 Indicatory
4 Catalogued	9 Percussion
5 Gingersnap	10 Alarmingly

Q18 One-word four (A33)

★★

All of the following are one-word anagrams:

1	Enumeration	8	Permeations
2	Adulterines	9	Desecration
3	Catapultier	10	Procreation
4	Inbreathing	11	Consumerist
5	Memorialist	12	Credentials
6	Enterprises	13	Conservation
7	Colonialist	14	Delicateness

Q19 Anagrams (A96)

★★★

All of the following are one-word anagrams. There are no links of meaning between the ten words and the groups.

1 Am a tall gray manic.
2 I, if Ada quit Colin's.
3 Present it to Martin.
4 Boy, I split rein sir.
5 Past idiot in tiger.
6 A green chain belt.
7 Leper's neat ration.
8 And suns grind time.
9 Mistrust ant Neil
10 The Martian island is in a bit mess.

Q20 Two in one (A80)

★★★

Each of the following groups of words contain two separate one-word anagrams of half the words in the group.

1 Stan dine built crest tuned meter.
2 I noticed boy spilt in faint I rise.
3 If I'm in a sly aged van, clip out oats.
4 I chart ice cap I print sheep carts.
5 Lift a coin call a timid ploy Issac.

Q21 Triplegram (A16)

★★★★

B and C are anagrams of A. A is a ten-letter word, each letter of which has been replaced by a number. No letter occurs more than once in each word. A, B and C are in alphabetical order.

A	1	2	3	4	5	6	7	8	9	10
B	1	3	2	4	5	6	7	8	9	10
C	4	5	1	2	3	6	7	8	9	10

Q22 Anagram blocks (A109)

★★★★

In each of the following there are six blocks of three letters. Unscramble all 18 letters to form a word, using all of the letters only once. No two adjoining letters of the word formed should appear in the same block, *e.g.* the letter 'Y' in word A would not adjoin the letters 'P' or 'E'.

A

I P A	P Y E
O O T	D S R
R I N	O T L

B

O P E	S C B
S H L	I N N
E E E	S R M

C

E T B	A M A
T I I	N N R
L H E	S A S

D

C C Y	A A A
H T R	C E S
I L I	T L R

18

Q23   Triplegram 2   (A54)

★★★★

B and C are anagrams of A. A is a ten-letter word, each letter of which has been replaced by a number. No letter occurs more than once in each word. A, B and C are in alphabetical order.

A	1	2	3	4	5	6	7	8	9	10
B	2	7	8	10	5	1	6	4	9	3
C	10	9	1	6	4	8	2	5	7	3

LOGIC

The only item required for this section of puzzles is your mind. The puzzles are purely exercises of logical thinking and require no prior knowledge.

Q24   Logic box   (A30)

★

Place the letters A, B, C, D, E, F, G, H and I into the grid of 9 squares using the following information:

A is above D and in the same row as I. B is above F, above I, and to the right of G. C is above H and below G. D is between F and H in the same row.

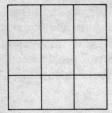

Q25   Logic box 2   (A86)

★★

Place the letters A, B, C, D, E, F, G, H and I into the grid of 9 squares using the following information:

I is in the same column as E which is not in the centre column. D is in the row below the row which contains F. A is in the row below the row which contains B. B is not in the first column. E is in the same row as F. C is in one of the four corner squares. G is in the square above A. F is in the same row as A, and in the same column as C. E is in the row below the row which contains B. H is in the same row as I, the same column as F, and is in a corner square.

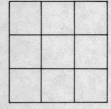

Q26 Smile please (A24)

★★

In a recent competition all 11 contestants lined up in a straight line to have their photograph taken for the local newspaper. So that the winner would stand out from the other contestants, the winner was asked to stand on a box in the centre of the line-up. Alec and Alma stood to the right of the box, Adam stood to the right of Alroy, two people stood between Aaron and Aubyn, Archy and Adrian stood to the left of the box, six people stood between Alma and Aaron, seven people stood between Alston and Albert, Antony and Adrian stood either side of Aaron and two people stood between Aaron and Archy. Who won the competition?

Q27 One missing (A100)

★★

Fit the nine small squares into the diagram to form a large square, each row and column of which should contain the letters A, B, C, D, E, F, G, H, I and J. What are the nine missing letters, and in which order should they be placed into grid E?

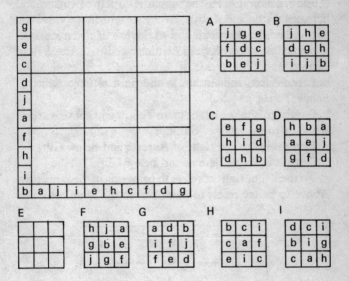

Q28   Paint puzzle   (A44)

★★★

There are 16 shelves on a wall which are arranged as shown in the diagram below. On each shelf there is a tin of paint, each containing a different type of Yellow. Using the following information, see if you can determine which type of yellow paint is on each of the 16 shelves.

Amber is below Fallow which is to left of Cream and Topaz.

Sulphur is below Buff and to the left of Primrose.

Cream is below Xanthic which is also to the left of Primrose.

Lemon and Guilded are to the right of Gold which is below Topaz.

Gamboge is to the left of Plain Yellow and above Aureate which is to the right of Sulphur.

Primrose is to the right of Aureate and below Gilt.

Saffron is above Lemon and below Gilt.

To the left or right of refers to paint tins in the same row. Above or below refers to paint tins in the same column.

1	2	3	4
5	6	7	8
9	10	11	12
13	14	15	16

Q29 The round table (A64)

★★★

Before King Arthur's knights sat down at the round table, they used to hang their shields on a rack as shown in the diagram below. Each shield was either red, white or blue, and was decorated with a circle or square, these again in either red, white or blue. Both rows of shields contained two shields and shapes of all three colours. No shield was the same colour as the shape painted on the shield itself. No red shield was next to, or above another red shield, but a red shape was above another red shape. Number one shield belonged to Bedivere and was white with a blue square. Number six shield belonged to Gawain and was blue with a red square. Number nine shield belonged to Tristram and was blue with a white circle. Launfal had a red shield with a blue circle, which was next to Mordred's white shield with a red circle. Calidore had a red shield with a white circle. Bors and Lancelot had red shields, Galahad and Percivale had white shields, and Pelleas and Geraint had blue shields. Percivale's shield was next to Calidore's and above Tristram's. The shield above Lancelot's had a circle the same colour as the shape on Galahad's shield. No blue shield was above another blue shield. To which knight did shield number 12 belong?

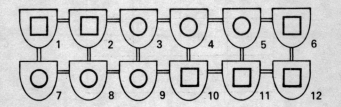

25

Q30 Clockwork (A74)

★★★★

Diagram A contains the first 23 letters of the alphabet and the numbers one to four. Imagine that the eight letters surrounding each number can rotate around that number clockwise or anticlockwise. To arrive at diagram B, each of the numbers has been rotated twice, except number one, which has only been rotated once. See if you can work out the order in which they were rotated to arrive at diagram B, and, if they were rotated 90° or 180°, clockwise or anticlockwise.

A

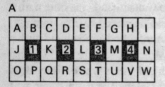

B

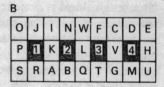

Q31 Laser (A8)

★★★★

The diagram below is a view looking down on a room 10ft square. The room has been divided into 100 smaller squares, as shown by the dotted lines. In each square there is a dot marked on the floor, or a double-sided mirror. When all the dots and mirrors are in place, a laser beam enters the room at A1 and leaves the room at J10, at the same time covering all of the dots in the room. When the beam reaches a mirror, it bounces off at an angle of 45°, as shown in square A3. Ten of the dots/mirrors are not in place; four dots (x), four mirrors from right to left (y), and two mirrors from left to right (z). See if you can work out what each of the 10 ?s should be replaced by: x, y or z.

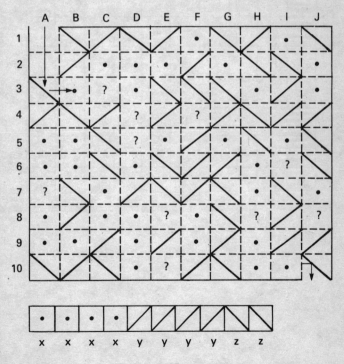

27

Q32 Mensa block (A92)

★★★★★

Complete the grid so that each row and column contains the letters

M E N S A B L O C K

					M				K
	K						M	C	
K			M				O		
				M		L		K	
					B		K	M	
	M			A		K			
			S		K				M
		N		K		M			
	E	M	K						
M			K						

NUMERICAL LOGIC

The puzzles in this section are, as in the previous section, exercises of logical thinking, with an added factor of numeracy. There are no complicated calculations involved in solving the puzzles and only a basic numerical ability is required.

Q33 Block total (A37)

*

Each of the five letters in the word block has a different value between one and ten. Using the totals next to the grid, work out the value of each letter.

B	L	O	C	K	33
B	O	K	B	B	33
L	O	K	K	K	24
L	C	C	K	O	34
O	C	L	B	B	37

35	35	29	33	29

Q34 A good year (A23)

★

Thirteen different years are listed next to the grid below. Using the digit totals next to each column and row, fit the 13 years into the grid, vertically or horizontally. Some of the years overlap, and each column and row contains at least one year. Two digits and one year have been entered for you as a start.

						9	27	1433
1121						1	17	1452
1189								1468
1194		4				4	19	1711
1232						3	26	1873
1272						3	13	1921
1426	6	19	16	21	20	20		1941

31

★★

Each letter of the alphabet has been given a different value from 1 to 26. Next to the list of words are the total values of the letters contained in each word. What is the value of each letter of the alphabet?

BEG = 59   CALL = 48   CHIEF = 36
CRAZY = 60   DEN = 53

GAME = 47   GUN = 51   HAM = 16
HAVE = 40   IF = 11

JACK = 24   KEY = 43   LAZE = 57
MAP = 28   MOVE = 58

NEON = 86   OXEN = 82   PALM = 47   QUIT = 40

QUITE = 60   STALL = 80   TALK = 39
TORE = 73   VAST = 51   WALK = 54

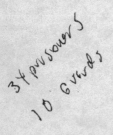

Q36 Safe and sound (A49)

★★★

The diagram below represents the layout of a new prison. There are 21 guards, 45 prisoners, six towers for the guards and five compounds for the prisoners. The towers are numbered 1 to 6 and the compounds lettered A to E. All of the compounds are triangular in shape and have a guard tower at each of the three corners. The number of prisoners in a compound is equal to the total number of guards in the towers on the corners of the compound. Given that there are 11 prisoners in compound A, one guard in tower number two, three guards in tower number three, and no two towers or compounds contain the same number of guards or prisoners, how many guards are there in each of the six towers?

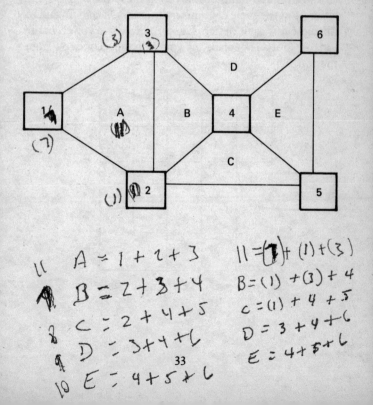

$$11 \quad A = 1 + 2 + 3 \qquad 11 = (7) + (1) + (3)$$
$$B = 2 + 3 + 4 \qquad B = (1) + (3) + 4$$
$$8 \quad C = 2 + 4 + 5 \qquad C = (1) + 4 + 5$$
$$9 \quad D = 3 + 4 + 6 \qquad D = 3 + 4 + 6$$
$$10 \quad E = 4 + 5 + 6 \qquad E = 4 + 5 + 6$$

33

Q37 'X' cluded (A84)

★★★

Number the letters of the alphabet A–Z, 1 to 26 respectively, then delete the letter 'X'. Using the information given, place the remaining 25 letters into the diagram. Three letters are already in place.

The totals next to the columns, rows and diagonal lines, are the total value of the letters to be placed in the column, row or diagonal line. The value of the letters U and F are 21 and 6, therefore the value of the remaining letters in the centre column is 22. The letter S should be placed in a square diagonally adjacent to the square containing the letter O. The centre column should contain three vowels. Place the letters Z, H and T in the same column. Place the letters G, H and I in the same row as the letter W. Place the letter M in the same column as the letters W and Y, and in the same row as the letters E and F. Place two vowels in the top row, but do not place any vowels in the second row from the top.

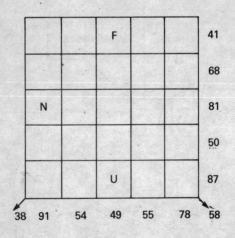

34

Q38 Pentagon (A76)

★★★

The whole numbers from 1 to 15 inclusive have been re-placed by letters in the diagram below. Given that A+D+G+J+M=B+E+H+K+N=C+F+I+L+O, the three letters in each pentagon total three-fifths of A+D+G+J+M, J = 1/3 C, E = 1/3 K, I = 1/3 N and B = 1/3 J: what is the value of each letter in the diagram?

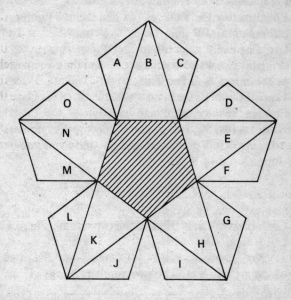

Q39 Numerical logic (A94)

★★★

The diagram opposite should contain the numbers one to six, six times each; the numbers next to the grid itself are the row and column number totals. Using the following 12 clues complete the diagram. (NOP means no other pairs of numbers.)

Across

A Contains two 1's, NOP, no 4's and the two numbers in columns E and F total 11.

B Contains two 2's, no 6's and NOP.

C Contains two 4's, two adjacent 3's and the two numbers in columns C and D total 5.

D Contains two 1's and two 5's.

E Contains two 3's, NOP and no 5's.

F Contains two 5's, two 6's, no 1's or 3's, the numbers in columns D to F run consecutively, and the numbers in columns A and B total 7.

Down

A Contains two 1's and no 4's.

B Contains two 4's, NOP, and the two numbers in rows A and B total 7.

C Does not contain a 1, 3 or 4. Contains four 2's, three of which are adjacent. The two numbers in rows E and F total 8.

D Contains two adjacent 1's, two 3's and NOP.

E Contains two 5's, NOP and no 4's.

F Contains three 4's but no 1's or 2's.

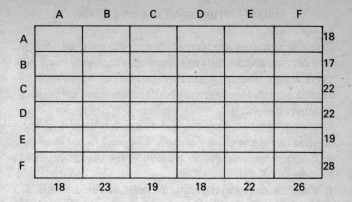

	A	B	C	D	E	F	
A							18
B							17
C							22
D							22
E							19
F							28
	18	23	19	18	22	26	

Q40   The old folks at home   (A6)

★★★★★

Last Christmas, a mystery gentleman gave a total of 276 gold coins to 23 residents of a home for the elderly. Each of the residents received a different number of coins. I asked the warden if he could remember the number of coins each resident received. The warden said he could, but, knowing how much I liked puzzles, said that I could work it out myself from some clues that he would send to me in a few days. I later received a letter with the following information included.

Maureen received the same number of coins as Brian, Colin and Arthur received in total. Vera and Walter received 35 coins between them. Una received the same number of coins as Gordon, Hilda and Ken received in total. Hilda and Lucy received 19 coins between them which was 10 more than Frank received. When the number of coins that Ken, Lucy and Joan received is added together, it equals the number Walter received on his own. If you subtract the number of coins that Lucy received from the number that Walter received and add the number of coins that Hilda received, it is the same number that was given to Vera.

Doris, Edward and Frank received 20 coins between them. Gordon received one more coin than Edward. Quentin received the same number of coins as Doris, Frank and Gordon received together. Gordon, Ian and Ken received the same number of coins between them as Thomas received on his own. Hilda and Joan received 11 coins between them. Colin and Lucy received 29 coins between them, which was 10 more than Brian, Colin and Edward received together. Vera received 13 coins, which was the same as Hilda, Joan and Ken received in total.

Five residents received the same number of coins on their own as another three residents received between them. Sally received the same number of coins as Hilda, Frank and Gordon; Norman the same as Edward, Brian and Colin; Olive the same as Brian, Doris and Edward; Rose the same as Hilda, Frank and Edward; and Peter the same as Frank, Edward and Doris. Olive, Norman and Maureen received 54 coins between them.

See if you can work out the number of coins each of the residents received.

NUMBERS

What is a number? The Greeks did not consider 1 to be a number at all. It was the monad, the indivisible unit from which all other numbers arose. According to Euclid a number is an aggregate composed of units. Therefore, as 1 cannot be an aggregate of itself, it cannot be considered as a number. Over the centuries, other numbers have had their problems too, including zero. During the Medieval ages, mathematicians could not decide whether zero was a number or not.

Today, with most of the confusion as to what is and what is not a number out of the way, we can concentrate on the characteristics of the numbers themselves. Most numbers have their own individual characteristic(s) such as 6174. 6174 is Kaprekar's constant, the result of Kaprekar's process applied to any 4-digit number, apart from exceptional numbers whose digits are all equal. If you take any other 4-digit number, and arrange the digits in ascending and descending order, so that, for example, 4527 leads to 2457 and 7542. Subtract, and repeat, the eventual result is 6174:

$$7542 - 2457 = 5085$$
$$8550 - 0558 = 7992$$
$$9972 - 2799 = 7173$$
$$7731 - 1377 = 6354$$
$$6543 - 3456 = 3087$$
$$8730 - 0378 = 8352$$
$$8532 - 2358 = 6174$$
$$7641 - 1467 = 6174 \text{ and the calculation repeats.}$$

6174 is also a Harshad number, because it is divisible by the sum of its digits. Apart from having interesting characteristics such as these, numbers can be fun. There are no one-star puzzles in this section and some may need a fair amount of calculations or juggling of numbers. Most of all be patient and you should eventually arrive at the correct solution.

Q41   Mini crossnumber 1   (A13)

★

Complete the diagram with six 3-digit numbers, using the following six clues:

Across
Row A A triangular number +1 (*e.g.* 1, 3, 6, 10, 15 . . . formed by adding 1+2+3+4+5 . . . .).
   B A cube number (*e.g.* 27 (3×3×3)).
   C A cube number.

Down
Column A A square number (*e.g.* 4 (2×2)).
   B A cube number.
   C A triangular number.

	A	B	C
A	1		
B			
C			

Q42   Jigsum   (A35)

★★

Fit the twenty pieces into the diagram opposite. When complete, all 14 calculations should equal the totals given next to the diagram. Each calculation is to be treated sequentially and should start at a square indicated by an arrow, then follow the direction of the arrow to the answer on the other side of the grid.

   There are six horizontal, six vertical, and two diagonal calculations.

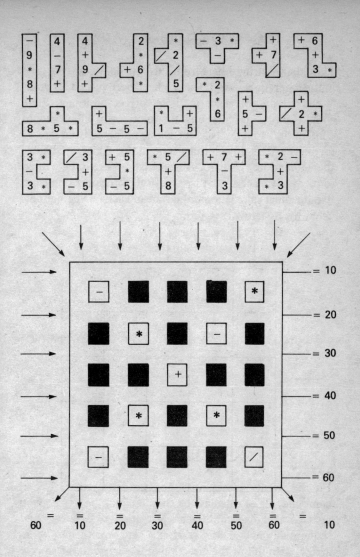

Q43 0 to 12 in nine (A48)

★★

Place the whole numbers from 1 to 9 inclusive into the gaps in the diagram below (3, 4 and 5 have been placed for you.) When all numbers are in their correct positions, there should be eight calculations, the solutions to which should contain the same digits as the whole numbers from 0 to 12 inclusive. All eight solutions contain two digits, are higher than 10 and less than 90. All calculations are to be treated sequentially. There are three vertical, three horizontal and two diagonal calculations, the start of each one being indicated by an arrow.

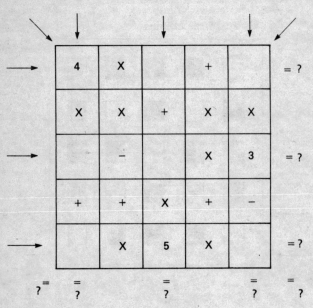

Q44 Mini crossnumber 2 (A108)

★★

Complete the diagram with six 3-digit numbers, using the following six clues:

Across

A A number which is both a square and a cube.

B A square number.

C A square number.

Down

A A triangular number (*e.g.* 1, 3, 6, 10, 15 . . . formed by adding 1+2+3+4+5 . . .)

B A square number.

C A square number.

★★

Add together five different numbers from the grid below to achieve the highest possible total. Starting at column A and working your way across to column E, you may only choose one number from each column, and no two numbers may be from the same row or diagonal line.

A	B	C	D	E
1	7	13	20	6
25	9	2	23	11
14	22	17	8	16
4	12	10	3	19
24	18	5	15	21

Q46 Prime crossnumber (A67)

★★★

The answer to each of the clues is a 3-digit prime number.
The clue for each number is the total of the digits multiplied
together.

Across		Down	
A	12	A	36
D	63	B	189
E	36	C	21
G	189	E	36
H	98	F	270
K	10	G	3
L	252	H	84
M	81	I	14
N	27	J	441
P	21	N	8
Q	48	O	162
R	63	P	63

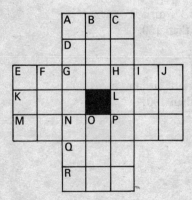

Q47   Connection   (A89)

★★★

What is the connection between 567 and 854?

Q48   Bullseye   (A21)

★★★

Three darts players playing 501 up have had three turns (A, B and C), each with three darts each turn. From the information given below, which player can finish with a bull (50) on their 10th dart?

Player 1
A   An odd score more than 70.
B   Scored 180.
C   An even number, more than player 3's turn B + 1.

Player 2
A   One score less than player 1's turn B.
B   Two thirds of player 1's turn B.
C   An even score more than 160.

Player 3
A   17 more than turn C.
B   The lowest even score of all nine turns.
C   An odd score more than 100.

Q49 Crossnumber (A61)

★★★★

Numbers finish at the thicker lines, no two answers are the same and 17 digits have been entered as a guide.

Across

1 Square   4 Square   7 Cube   9 Prime   10 Prime
11 Cube   12 Square   14 Square   15 Square   16 Cube
19 Square   22 Square   24 Prime   25 Prime   26 Prime
27 Prime   28 Square   29 Square

Down

2 Square   3 Square   4 Prime   5 Square   6 Prime
7 Cube   8 Cube   10 Square   13 Cube   17 Prime
18 Square   19 Square   20 Prime   21 Square   23 Prime
25 Prime

Q50   Number sequence   (A97)

★★★★

What is the missing number?

        1980   2961   3870   ?   9108

Q51   Number sequence 2   (A79)

★★★★

What is the next number in this sequence?

1   6   18   40   35   66   112   176   117   190   286   408   ?

WORDS

The puzzles in this section are word-based only. Although most can be solved without the use of a dictionary, others require some general knowledge.

Q52   All in line   (A53)

★

Find a 3-letter word that can be prefixed by all of the following letters to form another word:

B   D   F   H   J   M   N   P   R   S   T   V   W

Q53   Ending   (A7)

★

Find the word ending that can be prefixed by all of the following:

B   CL   D   H   J   L   M   PL   R   S   SL   T   TH

Q54   Which word?   (A17)

★★

Which word is the odd one out?

BYE   CAN   GEE   PAW   POT   TAM   TAR   TOM

Q55   Allsorts   (A104)

★★

Arrange the following into groups of four:

ALERTING   NITRATES
ARGENTIC   REACTING
CATERING   REAGENTS
CREATING   RELATING
ESTRANGE   SERGEANT
GREATENS   STRAITEN
INTEGRAL   TERTIANS
INTREATS   TRIANGLE

Q56   Prefix   (A81)

In each of the following, find a word which can prefix all of the words in each group to form another word.

★★ 1 Rhyme, Stalk, Water.
★★ 2 Brush, Frame, Tight.
★★ 3 Plate, Straw, Table.
★★ 4 Bark, Dish, Less, Root, Wort.
★★ 5 Body, Day, Time, Ways, What.
★★ 6 Able, Book, Over, Port, Word.
★★ 7 Boy, Flower, Point, Room.
★★★ 8 Bench, Let, On, Runner, Wise.
★★★ 9 Land, Penny, Plate, Pole, Weed, Word.
★★★ 10 Dog, Fish, Light, Sail, Shade.
★★★ 11 Brain, Down, Jaw, Pot, Rope, Up.
★★★ 12 Age, Ball, Berry, Bind, Bottle, Brash, Ice, Pipe.

Q57 Letter blocks (A73)

***

Arrange the following 36 blocks, each containing two letters, to form 12 six-letter words. The initial letters of the 12 words are:

A B D E F H L O P R T W

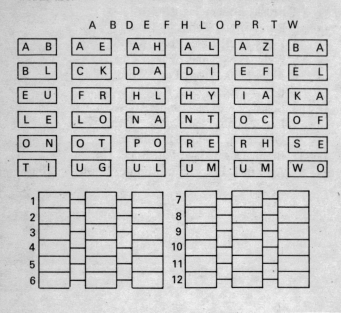

Q58 Mr Hoan (A106)

***

Mr Hoan has eight favourite letters, six of which are H, L, S, P, N and M. What are Mr Hoan's two other favourite letters?

Q59 Group puzzle (A99)

★★★

Arrange the following words into groups of three:

ABLE	HERB	SELF
BACK	KING	SLAP
DISC	OVER	STAR
FEAT	PING	THIN
FREE	RAIN	TING

Q60 Group puzzle 2 (A87)

★★★★

Arrange the following into collective(!) groups of three:

Bitterns	Poultry
Cubs	Quails
Curlews	Roes
Cranes	Seals
Fish	Swans
Goats	Teal
Herons	Whales
Pigs	Whelps
Pochards	Widgeon

Q61 What's in a name? (A101)

★★★★

Arrange the following into three groups of three:

COLIN FRANK HAZEL ELLEN GLEN
BERYL RALPH RUBY DOUGLAS

Q62 Qwerty (A9)

★★★★★

What are the two longest words that can be typed using the top row of the typewriter keyboard?

LETTER GRIDS

In each of the 12 letter grids on the following pages a number of words are hidden. The subject on which the words are based, and the number of words to find is given above the grid. The words may be found vertically, horizontally, diagonally, forwards or backwards, but always in a straight line. When all of the words have been found, the unused letters, when read conventionally, will reveal a word or sentence connected with the subject of the letter grid.

Q63   Letter grid—capitals   (A45)

★★

Find 31 capitals of various countries, and reveal another capital.

```
T  O  C  A  N  N  E  I  V  L  M  O  K  A
S  R  T  P  F  N  B  I  M  L  U  I  H  I
E  A  E  U  R  O  E  E  O  A  V  O  S  N
P  N  L  E  P  N  L  H  L  A  D  L  E  U
A  G  B  I  T  A  K  A  J  G  A  R  H  S
D  O  S  I  S  C  M  K  U  M  R  S  I  B
U  O  A  U  O  B  Y  S  A  K  I  A  U  D
B  N  R  T  C  E  U  B  T  D  U  J  D  A
E  E  S  A  R  S  A  R  A  E  U  N  W  E
J  H  I  A  A  D  A  G  Y  M  R  A  A  N
A  R  B  I  N  I  O  M  B  G  T  D  N  A
O  A  G  A  F  M  E  U  A  T  E  L  A  M
T  O  U  O  N  A  R  R  O  D  N  A  G  M
N  L  S  G  N  A  Y  G  N  O  Y  P  A  A
```

Q64 Letter grid—vehicles (A65)

★★

Find 28 types of vehicle, and reveal a vehicle name which is usually shortened.

```
A  P  Y  N  C  R  A  C  E  L  B  B  U  B
K  M  A  E  E  A  O  E  W  T  U  N  A  R
I  V  B  D  R  A  B  A  E  L  A  A  A  B
O  Q  N  U  C  R  H  L  L  D  D  E  A  R
R  E  U  H  L  S  U  D  E  W  L  C  S  E
T  M  E  A  K  A  O  S  A  C  M  B  C  T
E  O  S  C  D  Z  N  G  Y  O  A  N  O  S
N  U  I  N  E  R  O  C  S  N  E  R  O  D
N  R  A  R  L  N  I  N  E  R  I  T  T  A
E  L  H  A  A  R  A  G  A  T  B  A  E  O
D  U  C  K  T  H  O  L  A  R  U  N  R  T
T  E  L  O  C  A  C  D  R  O  S  K  Y  T
```

Q65 Letter grid—dogs (A91)

★★

Find 25 types/breed of dog, and reveal the last word of a quotation attributed to Aldous Huxley (1894–1963).
'To his dog, every man is . . . .'

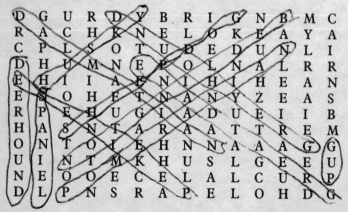

58

**

Find 26 types of hats, and reveal a line from a song connected with hats.

```
P  W  H  E  N  G  L  E  N  G  A  R  R  Y
A  R  R  A  O  I  V  T  I  L  E  R  E  D
N  R  A  E  S  B  K  E  P  I  E  Y  E  L
A  A  V  L  T  U  Y  N  M  L  B  E  Y  H
M  S  C  E  E  S  I  W  S  R  R  O  H  P
A  O  A  T  T  K  F  O  U  S  E  M  A  P
T  M  L  E  S  E  B  B  T  T  B  R  E  T
R  B  L  N  Z  T  D  A  A  U  E  A  E  S
I  R  A  O  H  E  L  O  R  F  K  R  H  A
L  E  B  R  R  K  B  G  T  E  T  A  E  P
B  R  T  B  E  S  M  I  D  I  K  Y  A  B
Y  O  Y  R  P  O  T  H  M  O  O  C  M  E
```

59

Q67 Letter grid—professions (A39)

★★

Find 35 professions, occupations and trades, and reveal an occupation which no longer exists.

```
R  R  L  P  R  B  R  R  R  E  R  A  N  R
A  C  E  E  U  E  A  E  E  E  S  A  M  E
S  V  H  I  R  P  I  L  M  T  M  R  D  L
R  S  O  A  L  M  P  R  L  E  N  I  U  T
U  E  E  C  U  E  A  E  R  E  T  I  I  N
B  H  X  T  A  F  T  I  T  O  R  L  A  A
S  O  S  E  T  L  P  O  R  E  E  I  P  P
R  O  S  S  D  L  I  E  H  R  E  I  N  B
C  E  M  U  O  N  L  S  U  S  A  R  E  A
P  A  K  R  N  L  I  G  T  R  T  L  E  R
N  L  I  A  E  L  M  A  I  S  L  R  N  E
I  S  V  M  B  A  I  S  I  B  I  G  V  K
T  V  A  U  K  N  T  T  O  U  B  P  O  N
Y  N  P  E  E  H  R  Y  Q  T  E  A  Y  I
E  R  R  R  N  A  M  S  D  N  U  O  R  T
```

Q68 Letter grid—dances (A58)

★★★

Find 24 dances, and reveal another dance.

```
T  P  Y  E  P  B  O  S  S  A  N  O  V  A
A  R  V  E  O  O  A  G  L  H  U  G  S  L
E  I  I  L  P  R  O  L  N  N  I  A  I  E
J  U  E  P  A  S  E  K  O  A  L  M  N  J
R  R  Q  B  U  T  H  T  A  T  D  I  M  E
O  V  A  S  N  D  S  T  A  P  R  N  P  Y
N  N  A  A  E  E  I  R  A  U  O  I  A  B
D  J  R  L  L  B  E  A  O  R  P  O  O  F
O  A  A  R  E  L  A  B  R  N  T  S  K  O
T  L  A  B  L  T  M  R  R  Y  T  S  N  A
E  H  O  O  U  A  A  A  O  A  O  B  M  M
C  P  S  K  T  J  H  E  N  I  U  G  E  B
```

Q69   Letter grid—groups   (A95)

★★★

Find 29 group names, and reveal the group name for apes.

```
B   M   S   N   S   K   U   L   K   F   L   O   C   K
E   R   U   D   O   W   N   M   O   H   L   H   R   C
V   G   O   R   E   I   U   W   M   O   A   U   L   D
Y   N   G   O   M   R   T   R   R   T   H   O   S   P
E   I   N   R   D   U   A   A   T   E   W   C   A   H
L   R   I   E   E   H   R   E   T   D   T   D   S   K
G   E   R   M   C   D   R   A   E   L   D   S   I   C
G   H   P   T   R   I   N   R   T   L   A   N   U   U
A   T   S   A   N   A   N   U   I   I   D   X   E   M
G   A   I   G   C   I   W   N   O   L   O   P   E   S
C   G   W   N   D   K   G   S   E   S   E   N   E   S
S   N   I   E   K   S   B   U   I   L   D   I   N   G
```

Q70   Letter grid—rivers   (A28)

★★★

Find 33 rivers from various countries, and reveal another river.

```
W   W   R   E   H   C   I   R   T   I   S   H   C
A   V   O   C   A   L   H   P   N   A   L   L   A
N   N   S   R   A   Y   U   I   P   I   A   O   W
G   I   E   Y   R   T   A   G   N   R   M   I   E
A   R   A   D   U   A   U   N   E   D   N   R   S
N   C   E   M   E   A   Y   N   E   N   W   E   E
U   K   A   T   D   L   C   U   I   T   D   I   R
I   Y   E   I   S   E   A   P   R   E   O   I   N
O   S   A   N   J   E   E   W   O   U   M   O   S
T   N   A   A   N   G   I   L   A   R   A   E   K
A   W   N   I   N   E   U   N   B   R   A   R   N
S   U   T   A   A   S   B   M   D   M   E   L   I
D   A   R   I   B   B   L   E   T   I   A   S   I
G   O   D   A   R   O   L   O   C   I   I   H   P
```

61

Q71 Letter grid—ports (A102)

***

Find 32 ports from around the world, and reveal a port in Egypt.

E	T	M	P	A	K	Y	F	I	O	S	A	K	A
L	A	U	O	I	D	L	O	A	A	D	L	T	E
L	L	N	V	U	U	A	Y	K	E	H	T	K	G
A	E	R	E	S	L	R	N	L	O	E	I	I	X
G	A	H	H	L	A	M	A	I	I	H	S	E	A
L	E	I	A	E	S	I	E	M	K	B	A	L	W
P	N	V	L	K	D	I	A	I	O	A	I	M	N
G	E	N	A	E	O	D	N	R	N	K	A	A	A
A	U	E	M	T	A	D	N	O	I	N	V	C	K
D	R	D	D	N	A	E	A	R	R	A	E	A	H
E	E	A	A	A	A	M	A	T	R	E	N	S	O
N	B	C	W	G	R	T	A	I	E	R	I	S	D
D	O	O	I	T	A	A	N	T	A	R	C	A	K
C	O	R	K	M	M	O	P	V	I	A	E	R	A

Q72 Letter grid—composers (A51)

***

Find 27 composers, and reveal another composer.

S	O	U	S	A	E	B	L	N	R	E	K	T
K	L	F	E	T	E	L	E	B	Y	R	D	C
O	R	N	F	L	R	V	R	K	Y	M	D	I
I	R	E	L	E	O	A	S	A	O	U	K	D
A	N	I	I	H	N	N	Z	N	E	S	C	E
S	N	I	T	S	I	B	T	O	N	S	O	N
I	U	E	T	V	L	E	A	E	M	O	U	E
C	E	I	A	N	V	E	R	C	A	R	P	B
B	W	R	L	E	O	A	R	E	H	G	E	E
I	T	E	R	E	Z	P	L	S	T	L	S	R
S	V	D	A	B	B	G	S	T	E	K	I	L
B	I	E	C	E	A	I	R	I	R	Y	N	I
X	A	B	S	R	Y	S	S	U	B	E	D	N

62

Q73 Letter grid—heraldry (A83)

★★★★

Find 29 words connected with heraldry, and reveal an appropriate quotation attributed to Richard I (1157–1199) in 1198.

```
F  D  D  R  A  D  N  A  T  S  D  I  S  E
R  H  L  Y  G  N  E  Z  O  L  U  E  T  T
E  E  A  E  R  N  E  L  A  D  T  T  E  N
T  G  B  T  N  M  O  R  T  I  E  E  L  A
E  N  R  A  C  O  E  E  N  T  L  M  T  D
L  I  A  O  R  H  R  I  H  O  A  G  R  R
L  R  E  I  G  R  M  V  R  C  N  B  A  A
E  E  R  O  A  R  U  E  E  I  T  P  M  G
C  P  M  N  E  N  D  L  N  H  D  U  R  E
N  A  I  O  I  N  P  O  E  T  C  R  C  R
O  I  N  C  A  O  Z  K  I  T  E  P  B  S
I  D  O  B  N  A  T  N  A  H  C  U  O  C
L  R  I  I  L  E  H  C  U  O  T  R  A  C
N  I  S  B  N  O  Z  A  L  B  M  E  R  T
```

Q74   Letter grid—biblical characters   (A14)

★★★★★

Find 67 biblical characters, and reveal a well-known letter sequence.

```
R S U E A H C C A Z H C E L E M I B A T
G A A B C T D B Z E M R A N T L L V F T
S A Z A D O K E A G A N E I M I I E E O
B U M Z E B U L O N D L L U N I T J V L
I P I A E A H A B R A E D U B S R U A E
R H A R L N I C E D I H S O I E I I S H
E Y J U A I D W G R S K A T R S N L A L
H D H M L D E A U N R U P I H C A L A M
C K U T O U M L H P H A L H N I A I Q S
A E K J O Y A E R C B A Z I I A R S A I
N P R O R M A S S E V A L Z H L H A S H
N E A A T N I H H H N B R E A P E P M O
E Z M S B A A T W R A O E T S H O M E N
S I J H H E N T E E U C C N I U S E O Z
A H A S V H L H A W H X H H Y M H L H N
M C I P O N T I U S P I L A T E A T E T
U L R J U S Z S E N R E F O L O H E E B
E E U A E A E S O H A I K E D E Z B U M
L M S B A R T H O L O M E W M O A B O S
L E H C A R U T H T A H P A H S O H E J
```

POWER PUZZLES

These puzzles are amongst the most difficult in the book. Nearly all will require the use of a calculator or mathematical tables, and a lot of patience. Although you may find them more difficult to solve than the puzzles in the section on numbers, you will probably gain a great deal more satisfaction when arriving at the correct solution.

Q75   Power puzzle   (A70)

★★★

Replace the letters using the digits 1 to 9 inclusive. Each letter represents a different digit. A, D, E and F are even numbers.

$$A C I D = B^F + E^F + G^F = H^F + I^F + D^F$$

Q76   Power puzzle 2   (A88)

★★★

ABCDEFGF is an 8-digit number. The digits 1 and 9 do not appear. Even numbers appear in ascending order, odd numbers in descending order. What are A, B, C, D, E, F and G equal to?

$$A B C D E F G F = A^E + B^E + C^E + D^E + \\ E^E + F^E + G^E + F^E$$

Q77   Power puzzle 3   (A43)

★★★★

ABCDEFGCC is a 9-digit number. The numbers 1, 2 and 6 do not appear. The odd numbers 3, 5, 7 and 9 appear in ascending order. What are A, B, C, D, E, F and G equal to?

$$A B C D E F G C C = A^A + B^B + C^C + D^D + \\ E^E + F^F + G^G + C^C + C^C$$

Q78 Power puzzle 4   (A22)

★★★★

ABB, ACD, AED, FBE and CEA are 3-digit numbers. Each letter has been replaced by a different number. What are A, B, C, D, E, F and G equal to?

$$A B B = A^C + G^C + C^C + F^C$$

$$A C D = A^A + C^G + D^C$$

$$A E D = A^G + E^G + D^C$$

$$F B E = F^C + B^C + E^C$$

$$C E A = C^C + E^C + A^C$$

Q79 The square cube   (A107)

★★★★

Find a number whose square and cube between them use all the digits from 0 to 9 inclusive.

Q80 Power property   (A34)

★★★★★

Replace the letters using the digits 1 to 9 inclusive. Each letter represents a different digit. F, G, H and I are odd numbers. When complete, 6-figure numbers with the same property, which no other 6-figure numbers possess, will be revealed.

$$G B I, G B E = E D B^D$$

$$A D B, A D F = H D H^D$$

$$H G A, H G C = B E C^D$$

HIDDEN MESSAGES

The first three puzzles are straightforward cryptograms where each letter of the alphabet has been substituted by another. The remaining three are different code puzzles, including a numerical cryptogram.

Q81   Cryptogram quotation   (A59)
★★★
Decode the following:

'LIH LRQH IMF ZDQH,' LIH XMKPVF FMRY,

'LD LMKS DT QMWB LIRWEF;

DT FIDHF—MWY FIRJF—
MWY FHMKRWE XMN—

DT ZMAAMEHF—MWY SRWEF—

MWY XIB LIH FHM RF ADRKRWE IDL—

MWY XIHLIHP JREF IMGH XRWEF.'

KHXRF ZMPPDKK

Q82   Cryptogram rhyme   (A78)
★★★
Decode the following:

YKH DIC, YKH VOZZ, YKH
KHIWHRZT YEURL,

IRX RHMY YKH PDIV, YKH ZUJR LKURHL,

YKH WUDQUR, IRX YKH LPIZHL,

YKH LPJDFUJR, IDPKHD, IRX KH-QJIY,

YKH CIR YKIY VHIDL YKH EIYHDURQ-FJY,

IRX BULK EUYK QZUYYHDURQ YIUZL.

(LUQRL JB YKH NJXUIP.)

69

Q83 Cryptogram limerick (A52)

★★★

Decode the following:

MTPSP'D K YAIXPSWRN WKUCNL GKNNPX
DMPCI

MTPSP'D BPSM KIX MTPSP'D PQQ KIX
MTPSP'D PCI;

BPSM'D QAPUD KSP ZRIH,

PQQ'D DMKMRPD KSP ORIH,

KIX IA AIP GKI RIXPSDMKIX PCI.

(BPSMSRXP DMPCI, OKGAZ PQDMPCI,
KNZPSM PCIDMPCI.)

Q84 Double quote (A66)

★★★

Two quotations have been mixed up below. All the letters
of both quotations are in the correct order. See if you can
unscramble the two quotations, the authors of which have
something in common.

WHGAITVIESOUURSTATSHEKTOTOOMAL

ASKEBARNIDTWAIENAFWITICOLULNFTRI

YNFOIRSHHERTOEHSTEOLJIVEOIBN

Q85   Code one   (A25)

****

Decode the following message:

15,1,6,36 78,15,153,153,15,171 45,105 210,36,45,190

91,15,190,190,1,28,15 36,1,190 3,15,15,105

171,15,136,78,1,6,15,10 3,325 210,36,15

210,171,45,1,105,28,231,78,1,171 105,231,91,3,15,171

6,120,171,171,15,190,136,120,105,10,45,105,28 210,120

45,210,190 136,120,190,45,210,45,120,105 45,105

210,36,15 1,78,136,36,1,3,15,210.

Q86 Code clue (A72)

★★★★★

Replace each of the letters in the following two sentences with another letter to reveal something which may help you solve a clue sometime. One of the letters has already been placed in a grid for you.

A	B	C	D	E	F	G	H	I	J	K	L	M	N	O	P	Q	R	S	T	U	V	W	X	Y	Z
						R																			

YAWC ITPYRCR OGNIN NUP AN IFLAH

____ _____ _____ ___ __ _____

REHTOEH TOTSDNO PSE RYLNO, EULC

_____ _____ ___ _____ ____

EHTFOF LAHENOO TLLE WGNITAL ERE

_____ _____ ____ _____ ___

LIHW, REWSN AEHTTA HTSNRAWT I,

_____ _____ _____ _____ _

TCEFFENI. GNINA EMELBUODA OTN

_____ _____ _____ ___

OITNETT AWARDO TSEHSI WDNAT

_____ _____ _____ _____

NELOVEN EBGNIL EEFSI RETT ESEL ZZU

_____ _____ ____ ____ ____ ___

PEHTNEH WDESU SIKRAMNO ITS EUQA,

_____ _____ _____ ___ ____

SEUL CDROW SSORCG NITT ESNEHW

____ _____ _____ ____ _____

WORD SQUARES

A word square is made up of words of equal length that read both horizontally and vertically. In most word squares the words are the same in both directions, but in some the horizontal and vertical ones differ. These are sometimes called 'double word squares'. The larger the square, the more difficult it is to compile. The largest word square made to date is a 10 × 10 square by Jeff Grant in 1986:

```
A P O L I T I C A L
P R O E M E T I N E
O O T S P R I N G S
L E S T U N N E L S
I M P U T I E R E N
T E R N I T R A T E
I T I N E R A T E S
C I N E R A T O R S
A N G L E T E R R E
L E S S N E S S E S
```

The word squares used in these puzzles are no more than 6 × 6 and most are 3 × 3. The final puzzle uses a word cube but it is not perfect. It would be interesting to see if a 3 × 3 × 3 word cube can be formed where all the words used form a different word when read backwards. I've provided the blank grids below, all you have to do is fill in the words!

Q87 Inner word square (A18)

★

Place the remaining 18 letters into the grid to form a 5 × 5 word square, the centre of which is a 3 × 3 word square.

A A A A C C D E E E H N O R
R R T W

C				H
			R	
T		P		
				O
	E			

Q88 All square (A98)

★★

Fit the nine squares together to form a word square containing six 6-letter words.

R E	T E	E R	T A	R T	C I	E S	T E	G A
T R	E R	S E	E L	E R	I B	R E	A L	A V

Q89 Word square links (A3)

★★★

Place the pairs of letters into the grid to form five 4 × 4 word squares. The four outer squares overlap the centre square by one letter; the four letters being P, E, E and Y. You may only place one pair of letters in each rectangle, and the first letter of each pair must be placed to the left of the second letter if you place the pair in a horizontal rectangle, and above the second letter if placed in a vertical rectangle. Each square reads the same down as across.

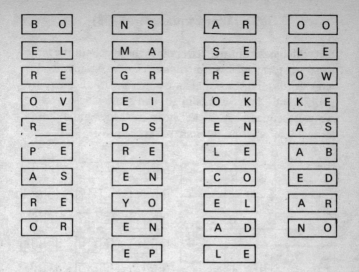

Q90 Word squares (A103)

★★★

Place the blocks of three letters into the spaces in the large
square to form four word squares. Each contains five 5-
letter words, and reads the same down as across. There are
20 different 5-letter words in all, and some blocks overlap
two word squares. A thicker horizontal line and a dotted
vertical line separate the four squares.

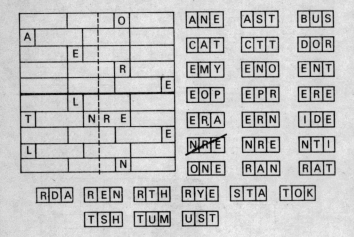

76

Q91   Word square grid   (A82)

★★★★

Place the pairs of letters in the grid to complete the cross-word and form eight overlapping word squares. The first letter in each pair should be placed above the second letter if the two letters are entered vertically.

AD	AK	AM	AP	AY	EE	EF	ER
ET	EW	FF	GA	GE	HA	IP	JA
LE	LY	ME	ME	MO	NE	NI	OD
OD	RA	RI	TA	TA	WR	YA	YO

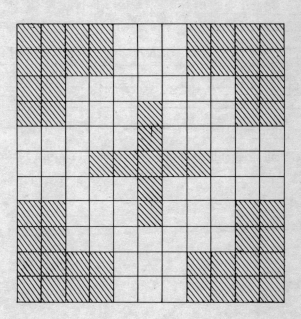

Q92   Word cube   (A75)

★★★★

Place the list of 18 letters into the centre and bottom grids to form two three by three word squares. Then place all three grids together to form a cube so that a total of 18 different 3-letter words are formed by reading any three letters in a straight line; *e.g.* when the three grids are placed on top of each other to form a cube, the top left-hand square of the top grid, the centre square of the centre grid and the bottom right-hand square of the bottom grid will form a straight line of three letters. Diagonal words in the word squares also count.

A   A   A   E   E   E   E   E   E   N   R   R   R
T   W   W   Y

| *TOP* | *CENTRE* | *BOTTOM* |

A	S	A
S	E	C
A	C	E

(Not all straight lines of three letters have to form a 3-letter word.)

MAGIC SQUARES

The whole numbers 1 to 9 inclusive can be arranged in a magic square so that all rows, columns and both diagonals have the same sum of 15. This can be done in only one way, all solutions being related by reflections and rotations to each other. The square shown below is the Lo Shu magic square, as it was known to the ancient Chinese.

4	9	2
3	5	7
8	1	6

The Lo Shu square has many different properties. All four lines through the centre are in arithmetical progression, with differences 1,2,3,4 rotating anti-clockwise from 654 to 951. The sum of the squares of the first and third columns are equals: $4^2 + 3^2 + 8^2 = 2^2 + 7^2 + 6^2 = 89$. The middle column gives $9^2 + 5^2 + 1^2 = 107 = 89 + 18$. The squares of the numbers in the rows sum to 101, 83 and 101, and $101 - 83 = 18$. Also, there are only 8 different ways in which 15 can be made by adding three of the whole numbers from 1 to 9 inclusive, each of these 8 ways occurs once in the square.

This section of puzzles illustrates how a basic mathematical form such as the magic square can be transformed into many different puzzles. The next logical step up from a magic square seems to be a magic cube, in which all the rows, columns and diagonals of every layer, plus the space diagonals through the centre, sum to the same total. This is impossible for $3 \times 3 \times 3$ and $4 \times 4 \times 4$, and it is not known if $5 \times 5 \times 5$ or $6 \times 6 \times 6$ cubes exist. The first $8 \times 8 \times 8$ was published in 1905, and a method of constructing $7 \times 7 \times 7$ cubes was discovered in the late 1970s. Before you start on the actual puzzles I will leave you with an open answer: 111. This is the magic constant for the smallest magic square composed of only prime numbers, counting 1 as a prime. All it needs now is the magic square—good luck.

Q93   Magic square   (A29)

★

Complete the magic square using the odd numbers from 5–35 inclusive. When all the numbers have been entered, all columns, rows and both diagonals should total 80. Five numbers have been entered as a start.

17			23
7			
		25	5

Q94   Squares in square   (A55)

★★

Place the remaining whole numbers from 2 to 17 inclusive into the diagram. When complete, all columns, rows and both diagonals should total 38. Also, each corner block of four squares, the four centre squares and the four corner squares should also total 38.

		15	
13			
			6
	4		

Q95 Diagonal square (A10)

★★★

Fit the 18 pieces into the grid opposite to form a magic square. When complete, all rows, columns and both diagonals should total 175. Some pieces overlap each other at the joints between the squares.

e.g.

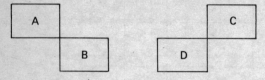

The pieces could overlap as shown below:

A	C
D	B

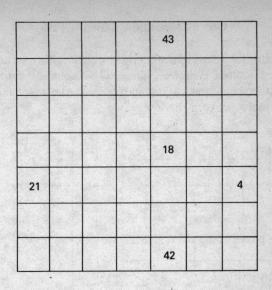

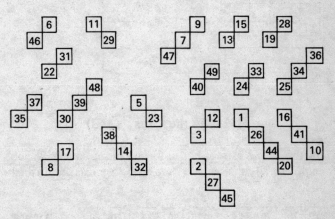

Q96 Magic square tiles (A46)

★★★

Place the 21 3-figure numbers into the grid, either vertically or horizontally. When complete, all the columns and rows must equal 45 when the numbers in them are added together.

168	195	247
261	357	437
438	468	573
575	624	627
683	733	816
819	848	924
924	951	953

Q97 All the fours (A63)

★★★

Fit the 14 pieces together to form a magic square. When complete, all columns, rows and both diagonals should total 444.

Q98   The bottom line   (A90)

★★★

Given that J = O, G = E + A, B = C + I, and D = B − G, and all columns, rows and both diagonals total 1000 more than the highest triangular number under 1000, what are the seven 3-figure numbers missing from the bottom line?

EBF	EHG	EFG	EBE	AJD	EFJ	EIF
?	EFA	EIA	AJJ	EHC	EFI	EII
EHD	EFD	?	ACJ	EHB	EIH	EBH
EFE	EIE	EBB	EHJ	?	EBD	AJH
EIJ	?	AJB	EHI	EIG	EBG	EHA
EIC	EBI	EHH	?	EBA	AJG	EFC
?	?	?	?	?	?	?

Q99   Grid zero   (A38)

★★★★

Complete the grid using the letters A, B, E and F eight times each, and the letters C and D 16 times each. All columns, rows and both diagonals must equal zero.

A = +25.132

B = −A

C = ½A

D = A − (6 × E)

E = ½C

F = ?

A						C
		B		F		D
		A				
C		D				
C			E			
F						C
B						A
	C	C			E	

Q100 Magic letter square (A15)

****

Complete the grid so that all the columns, rows and both diagonals equal A, and the grid contains the letters K–Z four times each.

$A = (P \times T) + R$

$Z = 2 \times R$

$N = V/3$

$T = Y - (N + K)$

$U = S + L$

$(M \times Q) + O + K = W + X$

Total value of $K - Z = 136$

K							
						V	
	O						
				M			
							W
		X					
	Z						
			N				

Q101   Magic cube   (A47)

★★★★★

Using the whole numbers from 1 to 64 inclusive, complete the four grids so that the columns, rows and both diagonals in A = 124, B = 128, C = 132 and D = 136. When all four grids are placed on top of each other, all 16 columns total 130. For example, 61 + 14 + 3 + 52 = 130. Twenty numbers have been entered for you.

A

61			
		41	
	21		
	57		01

B

14			62
	22		
		42	
02			

C

03	55		
47			
			19
		11	

D

52		48	
			56
12			
	20		

CROSSWORDS

In this final section all puzzles are based on the crossword, probably the most common and well-known puzzle to date. There is no 'normal' crossword included in the section but all of the puzzles are 'crossword based'.

★★

Fit the letters into the blank crossword grid to form 48 different 3-letter words. The letters have been placed next to the row in which they fit. The letters have also been placed under the column in which they fit.

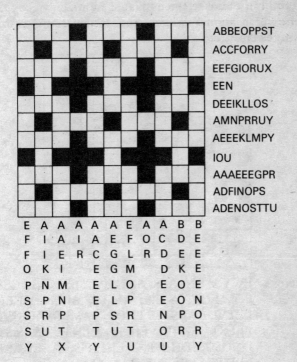

ABBEOPPST
ACCFORRY
EEFGIORUX
EEN
DEEIKLLOS
AMNPRRUY
AEEEKLMPY
IOU
AAAEEEGPR
ADFINOPS
ADENOSTTU

E	A	A	A	A		A	E	A	A	B	B
F	I	A	I	A		E	F	O	C	D	E
F	I	E	R	C		G	L	R	D	E	E
O	K	I		E		G	M		D	K	E
P	N	M		E		L	O		E	O	E
S	P	N		E		L	P		E	O	N
S	R	P		P		S	R		N	P	O
S	U	T		T		U	T		O	R	R
Y	X			Y			U		U		Y

★★

The following crossword has no clues, but you have the
answers in front of you. Unfortunately, none of the answers
are numbered, and the letters of the words that fit across the
crossword have been arranged into alphabetical order. See
if you can complete the crossword by unscrambling the
letters of the words that read across, then placing the words
into the crossword grid.

Across   EWY, ADN, APS, AET, ESU, ESS, EIL, CES,
IST, EOT, AALS, ALMT, ABEN, ACEL,
EETW, ARST, EHOS, AMRS, EHIST,
EELST, EISTX, EILST, EENTV, AEMST,
DNOSU, DHIRT, AEHLRSS, AAELMST,
EEEIPRSTX, ACEFLLLSU.

Down   ECU, STY, NEW, COS, URE, PHI, ANE,
AIL, ILL, ULE, EFT, ATE, STAR, NETT,
BEAM, REST, SEAT, LESS, ELSE, ANEW,
SLEET, TERMS, THEFT, SPICE, HASTE,
DEALT,   DREAM,   LEAPS,   ESCAPER,
METRICS, VALENTINE, ALONGSIDE.

Q104   Three too many   (A5)

★★★

Delete three of the letters in each square to reveal a crossword with ten interlocking words.

YA UB	EH CO	RL NS	LW EA	RA VI	ZP MT	BC HE
AC BD		PY OA			LG FA	
PR US	NT OE	GM KS	EQ GU	HG MF	PU CH	BS TR
LJ UT		EJ FV		LA ZT		GI RO
GK QJ	IY MN	FD HT	PS ID	ES IA	PR YN	GI AU
	LU KY			QY JZ		BH CG
OK CB	SL TR	RI ED	KM LO	PR AE	IO JN	TE RG

Q105   ABC crossword   (A56)

★★★

The clues given for the crossword below are the answers in a coded form. Each digit of the clue represents two or three different letters of the alphabet as shown in the table below; *e.g.*:

(A) Across '3382', could be 'HIVE', derived from:

(G, H or I) + (G, H or I) + (V, W or X) + (D, E or F)

   H   +   I + V   +   E

Across

a 3382 **d** 2177265 **g** 1855 **h** 77562 **i** 1421826
k 22137 **l** 7578377 **n** 5333781713515 **q** 1337172
s 53779 **t** 6475132 **u** 73567 **v** 5513 **w** 1425257
x 2556

Down

a 317326353 **b** 8165373 **c** 282 **d** 2515761325257
e 7126731 **f** 25853 **j** 657 **m** 711772626 **o** 7211142
p 3233335 **q** 146 **r** 35762 **u** 712

1	A	B	C
2	D	E	F
3	G	H	I
4	J	K	L
5	M	N	O
6	P	Q	R
7	S	T	U
8	V	W	X
9	Y	Z	–

Q106 Crossbits (A40)

***

Fit the 25 pieces together to form a symmetrical crossword.

	T	O
O	R	
	O	

	O	
	L	E
A	L	

P	O	R
	U	
S	T	A

E	N	T
A		Y
L	L	

	T	I
A		N
B	I	C

	E	T
	A	
E	F	L

E		U
A		N
T	O	T

H	O	S
	A	
A	T	E

O		A
R		
A	R	R

U	C	H
S		E
E		A

H	R	A
		R
E	A	C

S		
S	T	E
		N

L	E	S
		E
D		I

T	O	P
N		
E	R	O

D	A	L
	N	I
	I	

E		S
S	S	
		A

	T	
	E	
S	M	A

T	I	O
I		
L	E	

B	L	E
O		W
A	T	E

	G	
G	R	A
	E	

	U	
R	G	E
	B	

N		C
E	R	R
A		O

D		H
D	G	E
Y		D

L		
	G	O
H		C

A	W	E
S		O
K	I	N

93

★★★★

Fit the 50 pieces opposite together to form two crosswords, each of a symmetrical pattern.

Puzzle grids (3×3 letter squares):

```
Row 1:
P R E    A L D    T S .    H U L    . A .
. O .    L O .    . H A    . M .    P R O
A B O    A M P    L Y .    S E N    . G .

Row 2:
. I S    I S C    E . O    . A R    R I V
. . E    N . C    R E R    E L M    . D .
D G L    T . U    . V .    L E .    S . A

Row 3:
. N .    . H .    W . .    S S S    . . I
A T E    . Y O    . D O    A . .    D U C
L . N    S . C    L . .    V E .    E . E

Row 4:
. S C    . L .    T I C    . N .    . B L
. C .    L E A    E . U    E P I    . L .
C H .    O . N    M O R    . A .    S E .

Row 5:
E E D    . O .    E A P    A . E    E S T
S . E    . O V    N . E    T . .    . . H
S A N    O L O    O N C    E X P    T . R

Row 6:
E . .    L E T    D . M    O V E    L O T
D D E    . N .    E . .    S . L    O . I
Y . A    A S S    S A L    E W E    C A R

Row 7:
T U D    O P I    . H E    K N O    . T .
O . A    . . S    D E .    Y O .    N U R
P A R    R . A    . A D    . B .    . N .

Row 8:
V E N    . . K    E . S    R . N    S . R
I . O    L Y .    R D E    . A .    T R U
I E R    . . S    Y . D    E T T    E . C

Row 9:
N . L    O T A    E . A    A D R    L . T
A D E    T . B    D E N    D . O    L . I
R . .    T C H    . . G    D U C    A T O

Row 10:
. Y .    E . E    T . E    O P Y    E V E
N E R    T E N    E R .    . L .    A . A
. R .    . M .    . O .    P O N    S I T
```

★★★★

The crossword below has had all its letters replaced by
numbers. Only nine different letters have been used in the
crossword. Each has been replaced by a number from 0 to 8.
Which letter does each of the nine numbers represent?

6		4	5	5	4	7	0	4	8	6		6	7	3
4	0	6	2		0			7		2		2		0
3		2		5	1	3		2	3	6	1	6	6	1
6	7	8	1	4		4		0		1		4		4
		4		0	4	5	5	7	1		3	0	4	8
4	0	0	2	6	6	1	1		8	7	0			
	7		5		6		3		6		7	8	6	2
	8		3	2	4	5	6	0	7	8	1		1	
5	2	0	7		7		7		6		8		1	
		8	2	8		2	7	0	5	6	2	8	1
0	7	8	1		6	7	8	5	1	0		0		
4		7		8		8		0		7	0	1	4	0
6	2	1	8	4	7	0		1	4	6		4		4
1		3		8		1			0		2	6	7	3
8	1	1		4	8	6	7	3	0	7	8	1		1

★★★★★

Fit the 75 pieces together to form three crosswords, each of
symmetrical pattern.

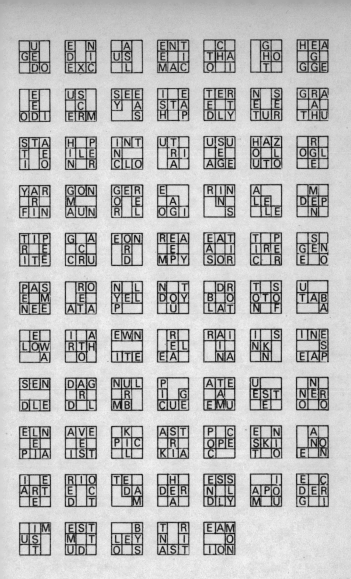

97

ANSWERS

A1 Sequence (Q10)

Between the numbers six and three. The numbers are in alphabetical order.

A2 Numbers (Q3)

A) 20. The sequence is the position of the letter in the alphabet of the first letter in the numbers 1 to 12 when given in full, *e.g.*: *ONE O* = 15.

B) 81. The sequence comprises whole numbers beginning with a vowel.

C) 32. The sequence comprises whole numbers containing the letter O.

D) 2. The sequence is as follows; there is one number between the two 1's, two numbers between the two 2's, three numbers between the two 3's and four numbers between the two 4's.

E) 205. $1 + 1 \times 2 + 3 \times 4 + 5 \times 6 + 7$

F) 70. Sum of digits in all previous numbers in the sequence.

G) 307. Difference divided by three and added to last number.

H) 4895. Each number is multiplied by its rank in the sequence, and the next number is subtracted. $9 \times 1 - 2 = 7 \times 3 - 4 = 17 \times 5 - 6 = 79 \times 7 - 8 = 545 \times 9 - 10 = 4895$.

I) 21. They all begin with the letter T.

J) 52. The numbers are the totals of the letters in the words ONE, TWO, THREE, FOUR, FIVE and SIX, when A = 1, B = 2, C = 3 etc.

A3 Word square links (Q89)

```
B O O K      M A L E
O G R E      A B E L
O R L E      L E N S
K E E P A R E L S E
    A R E A
    R E I S
C O R E A S Y O R E
O V E N      O P E N
R E D O      R E A D
E N O W      E N D S
```

A4 One-word two (Q16)

1 Emaciated; 2 Direction; 3 Tailoring; 4 Personate;
5 Uncertain; 6 Variously; 7 Eradicate; 8 Organised;
9 Cessation; 10 Calibrate; 11 Insomniac; 12 Incognito;
13 Medicinal; 14 Schematic; 15 Astringed; 16 Lamenting;
17 Diligence; 18 Continual

A5 Three too many (Q104)

B	E	N	E	A	T	H
A		A			A	
U	N	K	E	M	P	T
L		E		A		I
K	I	D	D	I	N	G
	L			Z		H
C	L	E	M	E	N	T

A6 The old folks at home (Q40)

ARTHUR 7; BRIAN 1; COLIN 15; DORIS 8; EDWARD
3; FRANK 9; GORDON 4; HILDA 5; IAN 10; JOAN
6; KEN 2; LUCY 14; MAUREEN 23; NORMAN
19; OLIVE 12; PETER 20; QUENTIN 21; ROSE
17; SALLY 18; THOMAS 16; UNA 11; VERA
13; WALTER 22

A7 Ending (Q53)
UMP

A8 Laser (Q31)
A7 = X; D4 = X; D5 = X; E10 = X; C3 = Y; F4 = Y; H8 =
Y; J8 = Y; E8 = Z; I6 = Z

A9 Qwerty (Q62)
Proprietory and Rupturewort.

A10 Diagonal square (Q95)

38	6	16	33	43	11	28
46	14	24	41	2	19	29
5	15	32	49	10	27	37
13	23	40	1	18	35	45
21	31	48	9	26	36	4
22	39	7	17	34	44	12
30	47	8	25	42	3	20

A11 Crossbits 3 (Q109)

```
P A S S E N G E R   R O A S T
E   M     O   E     E       R
N E E D L E R   L A T A K I A
N   L   E   S E E   R   E   C
Y E L L O W Y   A   E L D E R
P       A       S E A   G   I
I N T E S T A T E   D R E A M
N   M   T   A   B   O       O
C L O U D   E M U L A T I O N
H   P   I M P       U         I
I L E U S   I   G E S T A P O
N   R   T   C U E   E   M   U
G R A N U L E   N E W N E S S
  A   R   D   I       N     L
T H U M B   E X C I T E D L Y
```

```
U S U R I O U S   T I P   K
  E   E   C   C   R   E P I C
A G E D   T E R M I T E   L
  M   I   E   E   T   P I N E
D E P A R T   E   I R E     S
  N   E   O D I C   R E A P
S T A T E   U   A     T   R
T   E   D A T A B L E   N   I
I   O   M     A   L E A S T
G O N E   N E O N   S   H
M     S K I   R   G E N D E R
A U N T   O   D E   O   A
  R   E N T R A I N   S A V E
O G L E   I   I   E   E   E
  E   M A C   N A T U R I S T
```

A12 What next? (Q8)

O It is the second letter in MONDAY. The sequence is the second letter of each day of the week in reverse, starting at Sunday.

A13 Mini crossnumber 1   (Q41)

1	5	4
2	1	6
1	2	5

A14 Letter grid—Biblical characters   (Q74)

Asa, Eve, Job, Lot, Abel, Adam, Ahab, Boaz, Cain, Esau, Jude, Leah, Levi, Mark, Moab, Paul, Ruth, Saul, Caleb, Enoch, Hiram, Hosea, Joash, Linus, Satan, Sihon, Silas, Titus, Uriel, Zadok, Andrew, Darius, Dorcas, Elijah, Elisha, Esther, Isaiah, Jairus, Miriam, Naboth, Rachel, Reuben, Samuel, Yahweh, Malachi, Meshach, Timothy, Zebulon, Gamaliel, Philemon, Zedekiah, Abimelech, Zacchaeus, Zephaniah, Bartimaeus, Belshazzar, Holofernes, Methuselah, Theophilus, Bartholomew, Jehoshaphat, Melchizedek, Sennacherib, Mary Magdalene, Pontius Pilate, John the Baptist, Nebuchadnezzar.

This reveals the alphabetical sequence ABCDEFGHIJKLM-NOPQRSTUVWXYZ.

A15 Magic letter square (Q100)

K – Z = 1 to 16 respectively.

K	N	X	Y	U	T	R	O
W	Z	L	M	Q	P	V	S
R	O	U	T	X	Y	K	N
V	S	Q	P	L	M	W	Z
P	V	S	Q	Z	L	M	W
Y	K	N	X	O	U	T	R
M	W	Z	L	S	Q	P	V
T	R	O	U	N	X	Y	K

A16 Triplegram (Q21)

A Perviously; B Previously; C Viperously.

A17 Which word? (Q54)

POT   All of the other words can be 'doubled' to form another word:

BYEBYE, CANCAN, GEEGEE etc.

A18 Inner word square (Q87)

```
C  A  T  C  H
A  W  A  R  E
T  A  P  E  R
C  R  E  D  O
H  E  R  O  N
```

A19 Clueless crossword (Q102)

O	P	T		A	S	P		E	B	B
F		A	R	C		R	O	C		Y
F	I	X		E	G	O		U	R	E
	N				E				E	
S	K	I		E	L	L		O	D	E
P		M	A	Y		U	R	N		R
Y	A	P		E	L	M		E	K	E
	I				U				O	
E	R	A		A	G	E		A	P	E
S		N	I	P		F	A	D		O
S	U	E		T	A	T		D	O	N

A20 Missing letters (Q6)

U and X. The 1st, 3rd, 5th, 7th and 9th letters are the vowels in reverse order. If you then number the letters of the alphabet A–Z, 1–26 respectively, and again 27–52 respectively, the letter between each of the vowels is the letter equal to their total in the previously numbered alphabet.

U	K	O	X	I	N	E	F	A
22	37	15	24	9	14	5	6	1

A21 Bullseye (Q48)

Player 3 From the information given, all you can work out is if the scores were odd or even. As only player 3 could have scored an odd score of 451 to finish on a bullseye, the solution is player 3.

A22 Power puzzle 4 (Q78)

A = 1; B = 0; C = 3; D = 5; E = 7; F = 4; G = 2

A23 A good year   (Q34)

1	7	1	1	8	9
1	1	9	4	1	1
1	4	2	6	2	4
2	5	1	8	7	3
1	2	3	2	2	3

A24 Smile please   (Q26)
Alroy

A25 Code one   (Q85)
The message reads:
'Each letter in this message has been replaced by the triangular number corresponding to its position in the alphabet.'

A = 1	J = 55	S = 190
B = 3	K = 66	T = 210
C = 6	L = 78	U = 231
D = 10	M = 91	V = 253
E = 15	N = 105	W = 276
F = 21	O = 120	X = 300
G = 28	P = 136	Y = 325
H = 36	Q = 153	Z = 351
I = 45	R = 171	

Triangular numbers are formed by adding up the series $1 + 2 + 3 + 4 + 5 + 6 \ldots \ldots$

A26 Number boxes   (Q12)
B.   Both A and C add up when read left to right and counting the right-hand column first.
e.g. 583 + 146 = 729
    715 + 248 = 963

A27 Crossword by numbers (Q108)

0 = L; 1 = E; 2 = O; 3 = C; 4 = A; 5 = S; 6 = T; 7 = I;
8 = N

T		A	S	S	A	I	L	A	N	T		T	I	C
A	L	T	O		L			I		O		O		L
C		O		S	E	C		O	C	T	E	T	T	E
T	I	N	E	A		A		L		E		A		A
	A		L	A	S	S	I	E		C	L	A	N	
A	L	L	O	T	E	E		N	I	L				
	I		S		T		C		T		I	N	T	O
	N		C	O	A	S	T	L	I	N	E		E	
S	O	L	I		I		I	T		N		E		
	N	O	N		O	I	L	S	T	O	N	E		
L	I	N	E		T	I	N	S	E	L		L		
A		I		N		N		L		I	L	E	A	L
T	O	E	N	A	I	L		E	A	T		A		A
E		C		N		E		L		O	T	I	C	
N	E	E		A	N	T	I	C	L	I	N	E		E

A28 Letter grid—rivers (Q70)

Allan, Avoca, Bann, Cher, Chindwin, Clarence, Colorado, Delaware, Dniester, Dunajec, Eden, Gatineau, Guadiana, Gumti, Hamble, Irtish, Kennebec, Kootenay, Loire, Lugendi, Niemen, Orange, Porali, Putumayo, Ribble, Swan, Test, Ucayali, Wanganui, Weser, Winnipeg, Yarrow, Yuruari.
The revealed river is the Mississippi.

A29 Magic square (Q93)

17	29	11	23
7	27	13	33
21	9	31	19
35	15	25	5

A30 Logic box (Q24)

G	E	B
C	A	I
H	D	F

A31 Cubes (Q1)
3 and 5.

A32 Crossbits 2 (Q107)

	A		S		R		H	E	A	D	R	E	S	T
P	R	O	T	R	U	D	E		D		O			H
	G		E		C		A	D	D	U	C	T		R
H	U	L	L		T	O	P	I		N		E	V	E
	M		L		I			S	E	P	I	A		A
S	E	N	A	T	O	R		A		A		S	I	T
	N		R		N		A	R	R	I	V	E		E
A	T	E		A		E	L	M		D		T	E	N
L		N	E	T	T	L	E			S	A		M	
L	O	T		T		D		M	I	S	C	O	P	Y
O		I	N	U	R	E				C		L		
C	A	R		N		S	A	L	T		U	P	O	N
A		E	V	E	N	T	S		E		S		Y	
T			I		O		H	A	R	D	E	N	E	R
E	X	P	E	R	T	L	Y		Y		D		R	

108

```
P R E S S S T U D   S C A L D
  O   A     O   A     C H   L   O
A B O V E   P A R C H   A M P
  L   E   A     K   O     T   E
L E A D E N L Y     O V E R
O   N     G     S O L O     O
O V E N   L E A P     I O T A
S   L A D E N   E D U C T   B
E W E R     O N C E   E T C H
  H   K N O W     E     E   O
  Y O Y O     D O D D E R E R
S   C   B   L     Y   A   V
T I C   B L E E D   I S L E T
E   U   L   S   E     E   N
M O R S E   S A N D G L A S S
```

A33 One-word four (Q18)

1 Mountaineer; 2 Neutralised; 3 Particulate; 4 Hibernating;
5 Immortalise; 6 Intersperse; 7 Oscillation; 8 Impersonate;
9 Considerate; 10 Incorporate; 11 Misconstrue;
12 Centralised; 13 Conversation; 14 Delicatessen

A34 Power property (Q80)

A = 5; B = 8; C = 6; D = 2; E = 4; F = 9; G = 1; H = 7;
I = 3

$183,184 = 428^2$

$528,529 = 727^2$

$715,716 = 846^2$

These are the only numbers with six figures which are a square whose digits form two consecutive numbers.

A35 Jigsum (Q42)

4	+	6	×	5	/	2	+	5	/	3
+	−	+		+		×		×	×	+
9	/	3	×	8	+	6	−	5	−	5
+		+	×	−		×	−	×		+
4	/	2	×	9	×	2	−	1	−	5
−		+		×	+	+		×		+
7	+	7	+	8	×	3	/	2	+	7
+		−	×	+		+	×	/		/
3	×	3	−	3	×	5	−	5	×	2
−	−	+		−		+		×	/	×
3	×	5	−	5	−	8	×	5	×	6

A36 Letter grid—hats (Q66)

Balaclava, bearskin, beret, boater, bonnet, bowler, busby, cap, coronet, deerstalker, derby, fez, gibus, glengarry, homburg, kepi, mitre, panama, peaked, shako, sombrero, stetson, tile, titfer, top, trilby.

The revealed song line is 'Wherever I lay my hat, that's my home.'

A37 Block total (Q33)

B = 8; L = 7; O = 5; C = 9; K = 4

A38 Grid zero (Q99)

A	B	D	E	D	C	F	C
E	C	D	B	C	F	A	D
D	E	B	A	F	C	C	D
C	F	C	D	B	A	D	E
C	C	A	F	E	D	D	B
F	D	E	C	A	D	B	C
B	D	F	D	C	E	C	A
D	A	C	C	D	B	E	F

Apiarist, artist, baker, ballerina, bellboy, bosun, bursar, chauffeur, costumier, editor, enameller, envoy, farmer, fireman, florist, hotelier, indexer, navvy, nurse, painter, pantler, publisher, puppeteer, rabbi, raftsman, roundsman, rugmaker, shearer, squire, stainer, tiler, tinker, typist, usher, vocalist.
The revealed occupation is lamplighter.

A40 Crossbits (Q106)

P	O	R	T	I	O	N		C		T	O	U	C	H	H
	U		I			E	R	R	O	R		S			E
S	T	A	L	E		A		O		O		E		H	A
	G		E		S	T	O	P		T	I	D	A	L	
G	R	A	S	S		N			A		N		N		
				A	E	R	O	B	I	C			I		
A	W	E	L	E	S	S			O		A	B	L	E	
S	O		E	S	T	E	R			O		W			
K	I	N	D		I		N	A	R	R	A	T	E		
	T		E	N	T	H	R	A	L		U				
	E		A		Y		R		G	O	R	G	E		
S	M	A	L	L		E	A	C	H		C		B		
E		U		O		D		H		E	T	H	O	S	
A		N		L	E	D	G	E		A		A			
T	O	T	A	L		Y		D	E	F	L	A	T	E	

A41 Two halves (Q11)

228 The letters of the alphabet have been numbered 1 to 26 respectively. Therefore,
$$F + R + O + M + A + T + O + M = 202 \quad \text{and} \quad F + R + O + M + N + T + O + Z = 228.$$

A42 High scorer (Q45)

99 (25 + 18 + 17 + 20 + 19)

A43 Power puzzle 3 (Q77)

A = 4; B = 3; C = 8; D = 5; E = 7; F = 9; G = 0.

A44 Paint puzzle (Q28)

1 Buff; 2 Gamboge; 3 Plain yellow; 4 Gilt; 5 Sulphur;
6 Aureate; 7 Xanthic; 8 Primrose; 9 Fallow; 10 Topaz;
11 Cream; 12 Saffron; 13 Amber; 14 Gold; 15 Guilded;
16 Lemon

A45 Letter grid—capitals (Q63)

Agana, Amman, Amsterdam, Andorra, Belgrade, Berne,
Budapest, Bujumbura, Cairo, Damascus, Doha, Islamabad, Jeru-
salem, Luanda, Madrid, Male, Maputo, Mogadishu, Nukualofa,
Ottawa, Pyongyang, Rabat, Rangoon, Reykjavik, Saigon, Salis-
bury, Seoul, Sofia, Stockholm, Vienna, Vientiane.
The revealed capital is Copenhagen.

A46 Magic square tiles (Q96)

1	9	5	1	6	8	3	4	8
6	2	7	9	2	4	5	9	1
8	4	3	5	7	3	7	2	6
5	7	3	6	2	7	5	9	4
1	6	8	8	4	3	7	2	6
9	2	4	1	9	5	3	4	8
3	4	8	9	2	4	8	4	3
5	9	1	5	7	3	1	9	5
7	2	6	1	6	8	6	2	7

A47 Magic cube (Q101)

A

61	09	05	49
17	37	41	29
33	21	25	45
13	57	53	01

B

14	34	18	62
58	22	38	10
54	26	42	06
02	46	30	50

C

03	55	59	15
47	27	23	35
31	43	39	19
51	07	11	63

D

52	32	48	04
08	44	28	56
12	40	24	60
64	20	36	16

A48 0 to 12 in nine (Q43)

4	×	7	+	9	= 37
×	×	+	×	×	
6	–	1	×	3	= 15
+	+	×	+	–	
2	×	5	×	8	= 80

| = 11 | = 26 | = 40 | = 19 | = 12 |

A49 Safe and sound (Q36)

Tower number 1 = 6
   ,,   ,,   2 = 1
   ,,   ,,   3 = 4
   ,,   ,,   4 = 2
   ,,   ,,   5 = 5
   ,,   ,,   6 = 3

A50 Age old question (Q5)
Edward.

A51 Letter grid—composers (Q72)
Arne, Bax, Beethoven, Bellini, Benedict, Berlin, Byrd, Cesti, Couperin, Cui, Debussy, Elgar, Ives, Kern, Kreisler, Mahler, Monteverdi, Mozart, Mussorgsky, Offenbach, Scarlatti, Searle, Sibelius, Sousa, Spontini, Stravinsky, Zarenski.
The revealed name is Lloyd-Webber.

A52 Cryptogram limerick (Q83)

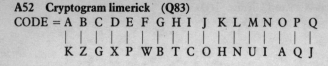

CODE = A B C D E F G H I J K L M N O P Q
       | | | | | | | | | | | | | | | | |
       K Z G X P W B T C O H N U I A Q J

       R S T U V W X Y Z
       | | | | | | | | |
       S D M R E Y F L V

The limerick reads:

THERE'S A WONDERFUL FAMILY CALLED STEIN,
THERE'S GERT AND THERE'S EPP AND THERE'S EIN;
GERT'S POEMS ARE BUNK,
EPP'S STATUES ARE JUNK,
AND NO ONE CAN UNDERSTAND EIN.

(Gertrude Stein, Jacob Epstein, Albert Einstein.)

A53 All in line (Q52)
AIL (All In Line)

A54 Triplegram 2 (Q23)
A Discounter; B Introduces; C Reductions.

A55 Squares in square (Q94)

02	16	15	05
13	07	08	10
09	11	12	06
14	04	03	17

A56 ABC crossword (Q105)
Across

a Give; d Eastern; g Avon; h Store; i Cleaver; k Debit; l Untwist; n Nightwatchman; s Misty; q Agitate; t Plumage; u Short; v Noah; w Clement; x Door

Down

a Gathering; b Varnish; c Eve; d Encouragement; e Sceptic; f Envoi; j Rot; m Scatterer; o Teacake; p Heigh Ho; q Alp; r Inure; u Sad

A57 Letter boxes (Q2)

1 O (October)
   N (November)
   D (December)

The box contains the initial letters of the 12 months of the year.

2 S (Scorpio)
   T (Taurus)
   V (Virgo)

The box contains the initial letters of the signs of the zodiac in alphabetical order.

A58 Letter grid—dances (Q68)

Arabesque, bebop, beguine, bolero, bossa nova, boston, charleston, fandango, hornpipe, jig, jive, juba, kolo, mambo, pookapooka, rondo, saltarello, saraband, shimmy, strathspey, tambourine, tarantella, tripudiary, valeta.

The revealed dance is the Paul Jones.

A59 Cryptogram quotation (Q81)

CODE = A B C D E F G H I J K L M N O P Q
       | | | | | | | | | | | | | | | | |
       M A Z Y H T E I R C S K Q W D J U

       R S T U V W X Y Z
       | | | | | | | | |
       P F L V G X N B O

Quotation reads:

'THE TIME HAS COME,' THE WALRUS SAID,
'TO TALK OF MANY THINGS;
OF SHOES—AND SHIPS—AND SEALING WAX—
OF CABBAGES—AND KINGS—
AND WHY THE SEA IS BOILING HOT—
AND WHETHER PIGS HAVE WINGS.'

(Lewis Carroll.)

A60   One-word one   (Q15)

1 Veritable; 2 Sectional; 3 Medicated; 4 Versatile;
5 Topically; 6 Reduction; 7 Simmering; 8 Laudation;
9 Stationed; 10 Tangerine; 11 Omissible; 12 Signatory;
13 Assurance; 14 Carnalise; 15 Centurion; 16 Ancestral;
17 Operating; 18 Nostalgia.

A61   Crossnumber   (Q49)
Across

1 5184; 4 6561; 7 125; 9 757; 10 31; 11 216; 12 3721;
14 1521; 15 8649; 16 6859; 19 2116; 22 7744; 24 937; 25 17;
26 701; 27 163; 28 3969; 29 6241

Down

2 1225; 3 4761; 4 653; 5 5776; 6 11; 7 12167; 8 512;
10 324; 13 19683; 17 877; 18 5476; 19 2916; 20 131; 21 1764;
23 409; 25 13

A62   Crossword   (Q103)

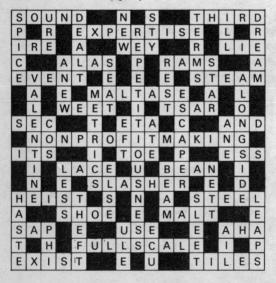

A63 All the fours (Q97)

144	8	12	136	20	124
28	116	36	40	104	120
52	80	88	84	68	72
96	56	64	60	92	76
100	44	112	108	32	48
24	140	132	16	128	4

A64 The round table (Q29)
Galahad.

A65 Letter grid—vehicles (Q64)
Ambulance, bandwagon, bubblecar, bulldozer, bus, cablecar, cacolet, chaise, chariot, clarence, coach, dennet, drosky, duck, hansom cab, landaulet, quadriga, rickshaw, roadster, scooter, sedan, surrey, tank, tender, train, tricycle, troika, van.
This reveals perambulator (pram).

A66 Double quote (Q84)
'Give us the tools, and we will finish the job.'
Sir Winston Leonard Spencer Churchill (30/11/1874–24/1/1965)
(Broadcast address, 9 Feb 1941).

'What is our task? To make Britain a fit country for heroes to live in.'
David Lloyd George, 1st Earl (17/1/1863–26/3/1945)
(Speech, Wolverhampton, 24 Nov 1918)

Both were at one time British Prime Ministers.

A67 Prime crossnumber (Q46)
Across
a 431; d 373; e 263; g 397; h 727; k 251; l 479; m 991; n 193; p 317; q 823; r 197
Down
a 433; b 379; c 137; e 229; f 659; g 311; h 743; i 271; j 797; n 181; o 929; p 337

A68 Letter value (Q35)

A	B	C	D	E	F	G	H	I	J	K	L	M	N	O	P	Q	R	S
8	25	2	12	20	4	14	3	7	13	1	19	5	21	24	15	6	18	23

T	U	V	W	X	Y	Z
11	16	9	26	17	22	10

A69 Words (Q4)

1 UNDERGONE. The vowels have been given the following values: A = 1; E = 2; I = 3; O = 4; U = 5

COMPATIBLE = 10   CURIE = 10

AUDIENCE = 13   UNDERGONE = 13

2 311. Position in alphabet multiplied by position in word for each letter gives the total value for each word when added together.

eg. SOUND = $(19 \times 1) + (15 \times 2) + (21 \times 3) + (14 \times 4) + (4 \times 5)$ = 188

A70 Power puzzle (Q75)

A = 6; B = 1; C = 5; D = 8; E = 2; F = 4; G = 9; H = 3; I = 7

$6578 = 1^4 + 2^4 + 9^4 = 3^4 + 7^4 + 8^4$

A71 One-word three (Q17)

1 Intoxicate; 2 Straighten; 3 Gloominess; 4 Coagulated;
5 Engrasping; 6 Instrument; 7 Emphatical; 8 Dictionary;
9 Supersonic; 10 Marginally

A72 Code clue (Q86)

Even though one of the letters has been placed in a grid, it does not mean that it is in the correct place, or, that the grid is of any use in solving the puzzle. The grid was no more than a distraction. If you write down the sentences backwards, the following appears:

When setting crossword clues, a question mark is used when the puzzle setter is feeling benevolent and wishes to draw attention to a double meaning. In effect, it warns that the answer, while relating well to one half of the clue, only responds to the other half in a punning or cryptic way.

A73 Letter blocks (Q57)
1 Absent; 2 Blazon; 3 Dahlia; 4 Eureka; 5 Frugal; 6 Hyaena;
7 Loofah; 8 Ocelot; 9 Podium; 10 Rhumba; 11 Tickle;
12 Woeful

A74 Clockwork (Q30)
Starting with diagram A, move 2–90° clockwise,
                              3–180°
                              4–180°
                              1–90° clockwise
                              3–180°
                              2–90° anticlockwise
                              4–90° anticlockwise

A75 Word cube (Q92)

TOP				CENTRE				BOTTOM		
A	S	A		N	E	W		T	E	E
S	E	C		E	R	A		E	A	R
A	C	E		W	A	Y		E	R	E

The 18 words formed are:
ACE; ARE; ANT; AWE; CAR; EAR; EAT; ERA; ERE
EYE; NEW; SEC; SEE; TAE; TEE; WAY; WEN; YAW

A76 Pentagon (Q38)
A = 14; B = 1; C = 9; D = 8; E = 5; F = 11; G = 13;
H = 7; I = 4; J = 3; K = 15; L = 6; M = 2; N = 12;
O = 10

A77 Division (Q14)
INCOMPREHENSIBLE

IRRESPONSIBILITY

MISUNDERSTANDING

MISPRONUNCIATION

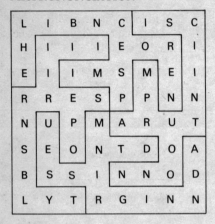

A78 Cryptogram rhyme (Q82)

CODE = A B C D E F G H I J K L M N O P Q
       | | | | | | | | | | | | | | | | |
       I V P X H B Q K U A G Z C R J F S

       R S T U V W X Y Z
       | | | | | | | | |
       D L Y O W E M T N

The rhyme reads:
THE RAM, THE BULL, THE HEAVENLY TWINS
AND NEXT THE CRAB, THE LION SHINES,
THE VIRGIN AND THE SCALES,
THE SCORPION, ARCHER AND HE-GOAT,
THE MAN THAT BEARS THE WATERING-POT,
AND FISH WITH GLITTERING TAILS.

(Signs of the Zodiac.)

A79   Number sequence 2   (Q51)
247   The 13th pentagonal number.

 1 = the 1st pentagonal number
 6 = the 2nd hexagonal number
18 = the 3rd heptagonal number
40 = the 4th octagonal number

The sequence then repeats itself to form a pattern with the 5th pentagonal number, the 6th hexagonal number, the 7th heptagonal number, the 8th octagonal number etc.

The following table shows the first seven of each of the above type of number.

Type of number	Formula	Number	1	2	3	4	5	6	7
Pentagonal	$\frac{1}{2}N(3N-1)$		1	5	12	22	35	51	70
Hexagonal	$\frac{1}{2}N(4N-2)$		1	6	15	28	45	66	91
Heptagonal	$\frac{1}{2}N(5N-3)$		1	7	18	34	55	81	112
Octagonal	$\frac{1}{2}N(6N-4)$		1	8	21	40	65	96	133

(N = Number, *e.g.* the 4th octagonal number = $\frac{1}{2}4(6 \times 4 - 4)$ = 40)

A80   Two in one   (Q20)
1 Indestructable/understatement   4 Apprenticeship/characteristic
2 Identification/responsibility   5 Classification/diplomatically
3 Advantageously/simplification

A81   Prefix   (Q56)
1 Eye; 2 Air; 3 Bed; 4 Soap; 5 Some; 6 Pass; 7 Ball;
8 Front; 9 Catch; 10 Moon; 11 Crack; 12 Corn

A82 Word square grid (Q91)

```
      H A M
      A G E
  T A M E N E T
  A P E     E R A
G A M E W   T A J A Y
A D O         A N I
M O D E E   W R Y I P
  E R F     R I A
  E F F L Y A K
      L E O
      Y O D
```

A83 Letter grid—heraldry (Q73)

Armed, Banderole, Barrulet, Blazoning, Boar, Cartouche, Chevronel, Couchant, Diapering, Embattled, Emblazon, Erminites, Erminois, Erne, Fret, Gorge, Hatchment, Herald, Kite, Lioncelle, Lozengy, Martlet, Naiant, Purpure, Regardant, Scutcheon, Sinople, Standard, Unicord.

This reveals 'Dieu Et Mon Droit'.

A84 'X' cluded (Q37)

M	B	F	O	E
P	Q	L	D	S
N	V	A	R	Z
W	C	I	G	H
Y	J	U	K	T

A85 Logic path (Q7)
91

A86 Logic box 2 (Q25)

C	G	B
F	A	E
H	D	I

A87 Group puzzle 2 (Q60)

1 Fish, Whales, Poultry (a run of)
2 Cubs, Pigs, Whelps (a litter of)
3 Teal, Widgeon, Pochards (a knob or bunch of)
4 Cranes, Bitterns, Herons (a sedge/siege of)
5 Quails, Roes, Swans (a bevy of)
6 Seals, Goats, Curlews (a herd of)

Some words can be placed into more groups but the above solution is the only way of arranging all into groups of three.

A88 Power puzzle 2 (Q76)

A = 2; B = 4; C = 6; D = 7; E = 8; F = 0; G = 5

A89 Connection (Q47)

$567^2 = 321489$
$854^2 = 729316$

Both equations use each of the digits 1 to 9 once each. These are the only two numbers with this property.

A90 The bottom line (Q98)

Reading from left to right:
289   308   267   284   301   262   279

A = 3		F = 7
B = 9		G = 5
C = 1		H = 6
D = 4		I = 8
E = 2		J = 0

All columns, rows and both diagonals total 1990.

A91   Letter grid—dogs   (Q65)

Alsatian, Beagle, Bedlington, Blenheim, Cairn, Chihuahua, Cur,
Dalmatian, Deerhound, Dhole, Great Dane, Greyhound, Husky,
Lym, Pekinese, Pointer, Pomeranian, Pug, Rach, Ratter, Rug,
Saluki, Schnauzer, Sheepdog, Spaniel.

The revealed word is Napoleon.

A92   Mensa block   (Q32)

A	B	L	O	C	M	E	N	S	K
O	K	S	L	E	A	N	M	C	B
K	N	B	M	S	E	C	O	L	A
E	A	C	N	M	O	L	B	K	S
S	O	E	C	L	B	A	K	M	N
L	M	O	B	A	S	K	C	N	E
C	L	A	S	N	K	O	E	B	M
B	S	N	E	K	L	M	A	O	C
N	E	M	K	B	C	S	L	A	O
M	C	K	A	O	N	B	S	E	L

A93   Letter sequence   (Q9)

N.   The sequence is the first and last letter of the odd numbers
starting with one.

The N completes eleven.

A94 Numerical logic   (Q39)

	A	B	C	D	E	F
A	1	3	2	1	6	5
B	5	4	2	1	2	3
C	6	4	2	3	3	4
D	1	1	5	6	5	4
E	3	6	2	3	1	4
F	2	5	6	4	5	6

A95 Letter grid—groups   (Q69)

Bevy, brood, building, cast, charm, chattering, clowder, down, exaltation, flock, flush, gaggle, gathering, kindle, lepe, murder, murmuration, muster, nide, pack, paddling, school, skein, skulk, smuck, sounder, spring, swarm, wisp.
The revealed group name is shrewdness.

A96 Anagrams   (Q19)

1 Anagrammatically; 2 Disqualification; 3 Misinterpretation;
4 Irresponsibility; 5 Prestidigitation; 6 Interchangeable;
7 Representational; 8 Misunderstanding; 9 Instrumentalist;
10 Antidisestablishmentarianism

A97 Number sequence   (Q50)

5823   When the reverse of the number is subtracted from the original number, the same digits appear but in a different order. These are the only four-digit numbers to which this applies (the exception in the sequence is 1980).

A98   All square   (Q88)

```
G A R T E R
A V E R S E
R E C I T E
T R I B A L
E S T A T E
R E E L E R
```

A99   Group puzzle   (Q59)

The 15 four-letter words can be arranged to form five 12-letter words.

BACKSLAPPING   DISCOVERABLE   FEATHERBRAIN
FREETHINKING   SELFSTARTING

A100   One missing   (Q27)

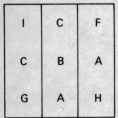

The small squares fit thus:
E G B
C F H
A I D

A101   What's in a name?   (Q61)

Frank, Ralph, Colin .....all types of bird.
Beryl, Hazel, Ruby ......all prefixes for colours. Beryl Blue, Hazel Brown, Ruby Red.
Ellen, Glen, Douglas ....all English rivers.

A102   Letter grid—ports   (Q71)

Adelaide, Cocanada, Cork, Damietta, Dunleary, Elat, Emden, Elsinore, Flushing, Galle, Genoa, Gisborne, Hakodate, Kakinada, Kiel, Kobe, Larvik, Macassar, Matarini, Moulmein, Mtwara, Nakhodka, Navarino, Osaka, Paradeep, Pula, Riga, Tamatave, Varna, Venice, Weihai, Yokohama.
The revealed port is Alexandria.

A103 Word squares (Q90)

C	A	T	E	R	N	O	R	T	H
A	D	O	R	E	O	P	E	R	A
T	O	K	E	N	R	E	B	U	S
E	R	E	C	T	T	R	U	S	T
R	E	N	T	S	H	A	S	T	E
S	T	A	L	E	P	R	I	D	E
T	E	N	O	N	R	E	R	A	N
A	N	E	N	T	I	R	A	T	E
L	O	N	E	R	D	A	T	U	M
E	N	T	R	Y	E	N	E	M	Y

A104 Allsorts (Q55)

The 16 words can be arranged into four groups of anagrams.
1 Alerting, integral, relating, triangle.
2 Catering, argentic, creating, reacting.
3 Estrange, greatens, reagents, sergeant.
4 Nitrates, intreats, straiten, tertians.

A105 Letter sequence two (Q13)

E. A is the first letter of the alphabet with symmetry about the
vertical axis, B is the first letter of the alphabet with symmetry
about the horizontal axis, H is the first letter of the alphabet with
symmetry about the vertical and horizontal axis, and F is the first
letter of the alphabet with no symmetry at all. The sequence then
repeats with the second letter of the alphabet with symmetry about
the vertical axis and so on.

A106   Mr Hoan   (Q58)
B and D.   Hoan is an anagram of Noah. If you place the word ark
after each of the eight letters, a new 4-letter word is formed. H, L,
S, P, N, M, B and D are the only letters to which this applies.

A107   The square cube   (Q79)
69   $69^2 = 4761$
     $69^3 = 328509$

A108   Mini crossnumber 2   (Q44)
7 2 9
4 0 0
1 0 0

A109   Anagram blocks   (Q22)
A Disproportionately; B Comprehensibleness; C Establishmentarian; D Characteristically.